ERNA BRODBER
AND VELMA POLLARD

CARIBBEAN
STUDIES
SERIES

Anton L. Allahar and Natasha Barnes
Series Editors

ERNA BRODBER *and* VELMA POLLARD

Folklore and Culture in Jamaica

Violet Harrington Bryan

University Press of Mississippi / Jackson

The University Press of Mississippi is the scholarly publishing agency of the Mississippi Institutions of Higher Learning: Alcorn State University, Delta State University, Jackson State University, Mississippi State University, Mississippi University for Women, Mississippi Valley State University, University of Mississippi, and University of Southern Mississippi.

www.upress.state.ms.us

The University Press of Mississippi is a member of the Association of University Presses.

First printing 2021
∞

Library of Congress Control Number: 2021946403
Hardback ISBN 978-1-4968-3620-5
Trade paperback ISBN 978-1-4968-3621-2
Epub single ISBN 978-1-4968-3622-9
Epub institutional ISBN 978-1-4968-3623-6
PDF single ISBN 978-1-4968-3624-3
PDF institutional ISBN 978-1-4968-3625-0

British Library Cataloging-in-Publication Data available

To Trevor G. Bryan (my husband);
Amy, Alma, and Courtney (my daughters);
and Allen III, Micaiah, Benjamin, Anna,
and Keziah (my grandchildren).

CONTENTS

Acknowledgments ix

Chapter 1. Woodside: The Lived and Imagined Homeland in
the Fiction and Poetry of Erna Brodber and Velma Pollard 3

Chapter 2. Velma Pollard's *Karl* and Erna Brodber's
Jane and Louisa Will Soon Come Home 22

Chapter 3. Spirit Theft and Spirit Possession
in Erna Brodber's *Myal* and *Louisiana* 39

Chapter 4. Migration, Return, and "Tomorrow's Spaces"
in Velma Pollard's Writings 64

Chapter 5. Erna Brodber's *The Rainmaker's Mistake* and
Nothing's Mat as Afrofuturistic and Speculative Fiction 80

Chapter 6. Gender and Identity in the Short Fiction
of Velma Pollard and Erna Brodber 100

Notes 119

Index 137

ACKNOWLEDGMENTS

This book is the result of many persons who have helped me strengthen and focus my ideas on sister-writers Erna Brodber and Velma Pollard and their re-creation of place through their use of myth, culture, folklore, and oral discourse. The sisters began to be recognized writers in the 1980s, a few years after Jamaican independence from Great Britain was established. Erna Brodber became known for the creative postcolonialism of her early novels, *Jane and Louisa Will Soon Come Home* (1980) and *Myal* (1982). Velma Pollard became known for her harmonious and witty poetry and short stories.

One of the many people who have helped me to strengthen and organize my thoughts after writing the book's first draft has been Vijay Shah. With great patience and writing skill, he not only read over each chapter with me; he also gave me new ideas of editing and focusing on key ideas and terms and strengthening the main premise. Before that, I began to work with several peers in academia, among them compatriots at Xavier University of Louisiana who took much time to read and comment on my writing as it developed and gave me support and critique. These included Professors Thomas V. Bonner Jr., Nicole Greene, and David Lanoue and his associates of our Critical Writing Group. Barbara Ewell, friend and English Professor Emerita of Loyola University of Louisiana, critiqued my writing carefully. My sister-in-law, Marguerite Bryan, a sociologist and former resident of Jamaica like Brodber and Pollard, read, critiqued, and researched subjects of my writing. My friend and associate Elizabeth Brown-Guillory, Distinguished Professor of Theater at Texas Southern University, heard me read several conference papers on the book and helped me to critique the work as well.

Overall, my husband, Trevor G. Bryan, JD, participated in endless days of discussion and reading my ideas and chapters as the book matured. His ideas are no doubt intertwined in this writing. And my daughters—Amy, Alma, and Courtney—as busy as they are with their own careers and families, offered me reams of support.

A final thanks goes to the critical readers of the book manuscript and to Lisa McMurtray, associate editor of the University Press of Mississippi, and the helpful associates who worked with me though all the final details of the writing.

ERNA BRODBER
AND VELMA POLLARD

Chapter 1

WOODSIDE

The Lived and Imagined Homeland in the Fiction and Poetry of Erna Brodber and Velma Pollard

Velma Pollard and Erna Brodber, two sisters and writers born and raised in Jamaica, re-create imagined and lived homelands in their work by commemorating the history, culture, and religion of the Caribbean. Pollard was born in St. Catherine, Jamaica, on March 26, 1937, to Ernest and Lucy Brodber. The sisters' father was a farmer, salesman of patent medicines, and community organizer. Their mother was a schoolteacher. By the time Velma was three, her parents had moved to Woodside, St. Mary, in northeast Jamaica, where her sister, Erna, was born. Even though they travel widely and often, the sisters both still live in Jamaica—Pollard in Kingston, and Brodber in Woodside. They write about their homeland, a series of memories, and stories of that lived and imagined experience in their many fictional, nonfictional, and poetic works.

The sister-writers create narratives that develop ideas of culture and place in rural Jamaica, amid the African diaspora. They center on their home village of Woodside in St. Mary Parish, Jamaica, occasionally moving the settings of the fiction and poetry to other regions of Jamaica and various Caribbean islands, as well as metropolises in the United States, Canada, and England. Despite scholars' tendency to look at diasporic literature from afar, this study emphasizes Jamaica from a local perspective in Brodber's and Pollard's works.

Indeed, Jamaica and Africa are never far from the sisters' writing. Many scholars have explored the significance of spirit in Brodber's work, including the topics of spirit theft, spirit possession, and spirits existing through time from the African past to the present.[1] Brodber's narratives also show communication between the living and the dead in many of her novels from *Jane and Louisa Will Soon Come Home* (1980) to *Nothing's Mat* (2014).[2] Yet, few scholars have examined Brodber's work on a par with her sister's writing. This study is the first to do so, drawing upon my original interviews with the sisters.

The world of the rural Caribbean and the metropolises that Brodber and Pollard visit consists of responses to their years of growing up in the village of Woodside. They contribute to our understanding of the region's culture and history. Growing up in Woodside provided a lens into the history of slavery and resistance, as well as the religions and folklore of the Caribbean, by which people of the diaspora struggled to achieve their independence.

The background of Brodber's and Pollard's works abounds with a sense of West African culture, folklore, and religion, such as Myal, Kumina, Pocomania, Obeah, and Vodoun. Along with spirits, Brodber portrays her interest in temporal progression and time shifts, so that characters often live in the present, the past, and the future. In Pollard's writing, there is migration from Jamaica to many places, as well as the search for placement and return. For instance, her novel *Homestretch* (1994) conveys the idea of nostalgia and "unbelonging" through a Jamaican couple.[3] There is also her poetry, along with her research in language and folklore. Her research includes the landmark linguistic study of Rastafarians called *Dread Talk: The Language of the Rastafari* (1994) as well as *Anansesem* (1985), a book of stories about the Ghanaian and Jamaican spirit Anancy, the title of which is derived from the Ghanaian Twi word. She has written five books of poetry—*Crown Point* (2003), *Leaving Traces* (2007), *Shame Trees Don't Grow Here* (1991), *The Best Philosophers I Know Can't Read or Write* (2004), and *And Caret Bay Again: New and Selected Poems* (2013)—and several newer poems published in various journals. She also writes short stories. Most of them were published in *Considering Woman* (1989) and *Considering Woman I & II* (2011, with new and old stories). She also writes pedagogical and scholarly articles about literature. Pollard has retired from the University of the West Indies, where she was the dean of the Faculty of Education.

Her sister, Erna Brodber, is a writer, anthropologist, and historian—she has called herself "an intellectual worker."[4] She has written five novels that are speculative and Afrofuturistic. The novels are *Jane and Louisa Will Soon Come Home* (1980), *Myal* (1988), *Louisiana* (1994), *The Rainmaker's Mistake* (2007), and *Nothing's Mat* (2014). She has also published several ethnographies, which are largely about Woodside, where she regularly holds her historical summer program called "Blackspace," and other books and articles. Brodber has also written short stories and published many of them in the collection *The World Is a High Hill* (2012). She has won several prizes for her fascinating postcolonial fiction, which presents her ideas about the past and future of the African diaspora. Her prizes include the Prince Claus Award (2006), the Musgrave Medal (1999), the Commonwealth Writers' Prize (1989), an Honorary DLit from the University of the West Indies at Mona (2011), and the Windham-Campbell Prize from Yale University (2017). She has been asked to speak and teach at many universities around the world as well.

This study of the literature of the two sisters from Woodside, Jamaica, differs from many recent studies of Caribbean writers because, as literary scholar Allison Donnell has suggested, there is great value in the work of writers like Brodber and Pollard who speak from a local perspective, since many contemporary Caribbean writers have moved away from their homelands and write about their homes from memory.[5] As Donnell writes, "The anti-foundationalist politics of postcolonialism appear to have generated a preference for dislocation over location, rupture over continuity, and elsewhereness over hereness." However, Brodber and Pollard provide detailed oral discourse, history, and folklore very rooted in the local.

Literary scholar June E. Roberts discusses Brodber as a writer of "interdisciplinary fiction."[6] Roberts analyzes Brodber's work in connection with the period of the writer's works and includes other Caribbean writers such as Kamau Brathwaite, Orlando Patterson, and Wilson Harris, but omits for the most part her sister Velma Pollard's writings. Roberts also considers only Brodber's first three novels, *Jane and Louisa Will Soon Come Home*, *Myal*, and *Louisiana*. By contrast, my study is distinct, for it thoroughly presents a comparative analysis of both sister-writers and on par with each other.

Woodside, St. Mary, is the source of much of the richness of the sisters' literary work. Brodber, an anthropologist, historian, and political activist, as well as a writer of fiction, has written several historical and sociological books about her home, which she finds characteristic of much of Jamaica. The first of these ethnographies was *The People of My Jamaican Village, 1817–1948* (1999), which she revised and expanded to become *Woodside, Pear Tree Grove P.O.* (2004). The second ethnographic book, *The Second Generation of Freemen in Jamaica, 1907–1944* (2004), was the result of Brodber's interviews of ninety inhabitants, primarily of the urban capital of Jamaica, Kingston, when she was a member of the Institute of Social and Economic Research. Another of Brodber's histories, *The Continent of Black Consciousness: On the History of the African Diaspora from Slavery to the Present Day* (2003), is a collection of seven lectures that Brodber presented in Woodside during her Blackspace "reasonings," ending with "Writing Your Village History: The Case of Woodside."[7]

In the introduction to *Woodside, Pear Tree Grove P.O.*, Brodber describes many of the inhabitants of the original coffee plantation, which became Woodside in St. Mary Parish. She depicts "the *creolization* of its Jamaican people, slavery, and development of the village and its inhabitants after emancipation."[8] In each ethnographic work and in her fiction, she examines the religious myths of her village and the development of the diaspora that has grown as people have moved to and from her Jamaican homeland and surrounding parishes. In *Woodside, Pear Tree Grove P.O.*, Brodber also explores her early life in the village. She says that her mother was a schoolteacher in a neighboring parish and was away often, although she would sometimes take Erna's older sister, Velma, with her. Since her father was a salesman of patent medicine and lumber, he was often away as well. Brodber was the second of five children, but the first to be born in Woodside. According to Brodber:

> All the others were helped into this world by Euro-trained health workers; I came in with the help of the local *nana*, Miss Rachel, a woman who looked neither right nor left and seemed to talk to none but God. They buried my navel string under the bluebell tree, a shrub that produced white bell-shaped flowers.[9]

The burial of her navel string in Woodside may account for Brodber's attachment to the spirits that presided over the area of St. Mary Parish in most of her fiction. She received the help of neighbors when her parents were away. "The spirits of Woodside kept me company and helped me to survive," says Brodber.[10] Sometimes she stayed with her maternal grandmother, who lived outside of the village, but she always yearned for the place where her navel string was buried in Woodside.

Pollard has been affected by literary influences in her family. In my interview with the two sisters in 2005, Pollard described her mother and father's influence on her writing and her mother's interest in poetry and language:

> "If I catch him, I mesh him" [in Pollard's poem "The Fly"] reflects the sound of the train I used to hear in Highgate. My mother spoke English; my father spoke Creole. My mother used book words. My father was into amateur dramatics. He would dramatize Shakespearean plays. . . . Father was a great storyteller. He loved to tell stories of Anancy. Both parents read a lot from the public library. We lived in a very rural area, but they read library books and sent them back by bus in a week. Dickens was their friend.[11]

Interestingly, their parents were steeped in classic British literature. In an interview with Evelyn O'Callaghan, Pollard said, "Both parents were involved in the local community—my father believed in 'socialism' in the truest sense of the word and was president of several societies as well as being instrumental in the founding of a community center."[12] The older couple in Pollard's novel *Homestretch*, who return to their home in Jamaica after many years in London where they tried unsuccessfully to find a better life in their "mother" country, emulate the parents of the two authors.

Both sisters left home to study at Excelsior High School in Kingston and then at the University College of the West Indies (later called the University of the West Indies at Mona, UWI). Pollard received an MA in Education from McGill University in Montreal and an MA in Teaching English from the Teachers College at Columbia University. After receiving her BA in history at UWI, Brodber won a Ford Foundation predoctoral scholarship to study at the University of Washington, in Seattle, before returning to Jamaica to study again at UWI in 1968 and then to join the faculty there and work with the

Institute for Social and Economic Research (ISER). She received her PhD in history from UWI in 1985.[13]

It was difficult for Brodber to return to Jamaica in 1968, after leaving the fast-moving times of the Black Power and Women's Liberation movements in the United States. She was wearing an Afro hairstyle and African attire, but most of the intellectual world at UWI did not understand the Rastafari movement, which was not at all accepted by mainstream Jamaica. The middle class and the faculty and administration of UWI did not accept Rastafari thought or reggae music, even that of the landmark singer and composer Bob Marley and the Wailers with sideliners Peter Tosh and Bunny Wailer "went on to attain phenomenal global appeal."[14] Brodber would soon join the Twelve Lost Tribes of the Rastafari, and Pollard would write *Dread Talk: The Language of the Rastafari*. While Pollard would adopt a more conventional approach than her sister, particularly in her primarily linear narrative, she still worked with concepts and language of the Rastafarians. The conflict between Rastafarian thought and capitalism emerges as a major theme of her novella *Karl* (1992), while her attention to Anancy and the influence of Ghanaian Jamaican culture are major themes of her short stories and poetry.

While working with the ISER and interviewing ninety older Jamaicans, Brodber wrote *The Second Generation of Freemen in Jamaica, 1907–1944*. She became a visiting fellow at the University of Sussex in 1981 and completed her study with the ISER for her PhD at UWI and later published her dissertation as a book in 2004. After publishing her sociological studies *Abandonment of Children in Jamaica* (1974) and *Yards in the City of Kingston* (1975), she went on to publish her first novel, *Jane and Louisa Will Soon Come Home*, in 1980.

Brodber presented her essay "Fiction in the Scientific Procedure" at the First International Conference on Women Writers of the English-Speaking Caribbean at Wellesley College (Massachusetts, United States) in 1988. In her presentation, she explains that she started writing fiction to make more teachable the ideas that she was studying with her sociology and social work students at UWI:

> Although *Jane and Louisa Will Soon Come Home* was intended to provide information such as Erikson, Mead, et al. had

given to students of culture and personality, I felt that my examination of Jamaican society could not be written from the standpoint of the objective outside observer communicating to disinterested scholars. It had to incorporate my "I" and to be presented in such a way that the social workers I was training saw their own "I" in the work, making this culture-in-personality study a personal and possibly transforming work for the therapists and through them the clients with whom they would work.[15]

Brodber's novels are case studies of the sociological problems that she was seeking to explain at the time. In taking this approach toward her fiction and study of sociology and anthropology, Brodber was carrying out her field study and writing fiction with an epistemology similar to that of Zora Neale Hurston in such works as *Mules and Men* and *Tell My Horse*. Hurston traveled to the southern United States, Jamaica, and Haiti to study African American folklore and voodoo/hoodoo by becoming a devotee of the religion herself. Brodber's first novel, *Jane and Louisa Will Soon Come Home*, was not meant to find a public audience. However, Brodber writes, "Velma Pollard, my sister, who had a long history of involvement with literature, felt the public ought to share it with my students and undertook to find a publisher."[16]

Pollard has written much about the migration from and return to Woodside and other parts of Jamaica, as in her novella *Karl* and her novel *Homestretch*.[17] In addition to her fiction, Pollard has written five volumes of poetry in which she describes her homeland but also many other parts of the Caribbean, England, and Canada. Although their narrative strategies in fiction are extremely different, Brodber and Pollard are nevertheless two sisters working with the same materials. They both write imaginative and scholarly works of rural Jamaica, particularly the history, language, folklore, and ecology of the place. Pollard's poetry and narratives are rich in the use of Jamaica Creole language and allusions to African and Caribbean religions and folklore but are different in structure from Brodber's layered, multivocal, and richly symbolic narratives. Nevertheless, both sisters write mainly about women and feminism in Jamaica after its independence.

Pollard published her first poem in 1975 when encouraged by her sister and others, notably Jean D'Costa, her friend and literary peer, who sent one of her stories to *Jamaica Journal*. Her poems and stories have been published in regional and international journals and anthologies. She is the author of two collections of short fiction, the novella *Karl*, originally published by the Casa de las Americas in 1992, and the novel *Homestretch* in 1994. In addition, Pollard has published five books of poetry, the monologue *Dread Talk: The Language of the Rastafari*, *Anansesem: A Collection of Caribbean Folk Tales, Legends, and Poems for Juniors*, and several pedagogical works.

Pollard's short stories, novels, and poems are set in several places besides Jamaica. The settings include Belize, Cuba, the British Virgin Islands, Guyana, England, the United States, and Canada. Most of her stories are about women and desire and what she sometimes calls "anti-love," which she defines as "when love is not."[18] Pollard explains, "No matter how you look at it, when you think about female identification in terms of a man/woman thing, you are in a cage."[19] However, she found encouragement in her sister and vice versa. Pollard says that when she was teaching in Guyana, she "wrote something that sounded, well, sort of 'goodish' [laughing]," and "I sent it to my sister [Brodber]. She showed it to Eddie [Edward Kamau Brathwaite]," and eventually, the poem was published.[20]

Pollard writes fiction stemming from characters and folklore of her home village, but her poetry is about many places, as are her nonfiction studies of language, particularly *Dread Talk* about the Rastafarians and Caribbean folklore of Anancy, the West African and Caribbean spirit. Music, poetry, and ring games, along with the oppression of women and the plight of their being caught up in "cages" of familial and social demands in the mid-twentieth-century Caribbean, recur as major themes in Pollard's short stories and poetry. According to Pollard, writing poetry and fiction, particularly short fiction, is a therapeutic and healing experience.[21]

The two sisters' imagined homeland projects Caribbean identity after years of colonialism following slavery. Both began their writing careers soon after Jamaica established its independence from the British Commonwealth in 1962, and they saw Jamaica as a growing diaspora, searching for its identity. They viewed their writings as allegories or metaphors for their community's coming of age. Both Pollard and Brodber invite the reader into their imagined and historical homeland, past and present. Their works give us an understanding of the Caribbean diaspora in its various facets, as Stuart Hall, the Jamaican-born cultural theorist, describes it:

> The diaspora experience as I intend it here is defined, not by essence or purity, but by the recognition of a necessary heterogeneity and diversity; by a conception of "identity," which lives with and through, not despite, difference; by *hybridity*. Diaspora identities are those who are constantly producing and reproducing themselves anew, through transformation and difference.[22]

Within this diaspora, history is important to all Brodber's work. In *Woodside, Pear Tree Grove P.O.*, Brodber lays out the history of Woodside, the village, its owners and inhabitants, and its creolization as New World diaspora. The village was settled not only by the diaspora born from the Atlantic slave trade, but also from the mixing of the first citizens, the Tainos or Arawaks, with the Africans who were brought to Jamaica as enslaved persons or indentured servants or who may have come independently as explorers and missionaries. People also traveled to Jamaica from England, Ireland, Europe, China, and America to develop farms or to start businesses. In one way or another, these diverse newcomers became a part of the area.

Brodber has continued her ethnographic writing along with fiction writing. The anthropological studies help students of literature understand the novels, just as students of anthropology are enriched as well. She began an anthropological study of her village of Woodside at Randolph-Macon College in Virginia and Gettysburg College in Pennsylvania in 1992. With students who visited Woodside in 1993, she collected oral histories, studying village traditions and the history of the area. Although the final product was intended for students at Woodside elementary school and local and former residents, it was published later as *Woodside, Pear Tree Grove P.O.*

Brodber's research points out some of the major people involved in the founding and development of the coffee plantation that became the village of Woodside. She also discusses the nearby properties that were leased to influential men called proprietors, who developed the land and contributed revenues to the British Crown. One of the earliest British proprietors of the Woodside area was Lord Bathurst in the 1700s. John Parker was another; he controlled the section called the Palmetto Grove/Louisiana area. In the eighteenth century, John Neilson began as a subcontractor but soon owned the land. A tomb in his memory remains in the churchyard near the plantation. Brodber discusses these individuals, "the myth of the body-less tomb," and "the myth of the haughty mistress" (John Neilson's wife) in the chapter "Writing Your Village History: The Case of Woodside" in her book *The Continent of Black Consciousness*.[23] These foundation myths, which she calls "two intertwined myths," were important to understanding the genesis of the village of Woodside.

The Neilsons were one of the leading families in the area, and their property gained a higher status than most of the neighboring properties. John was a major in the British regiment that settled in St. Mary Parish. He controlled about a thousand acres of land that became a major coffee-producing estate. When he married Frances Maidstone, she had a red carpet laid for the wedding, as Brober writes,

> that spread from a gate called "pillar gate" for about two chains to the present site of the Anglican church which was where the house she was to live in was situated. She was so haughty that she had to put on gloves to take money from her slaves. However, she came down so low that she had to walk about the district with a calabash bowl begging salt from her ex-slaves.[24]

Unfortunately, Frances's husband died at sea; she built a monument for him at the church, but everybody knew that his body was not in the monument. Later, their son, William John, became a medical doctor in England and acquired the land. He came back to Jamaica and married Jane Eliza, who had six children before his death at a young age. She buried him in his father's body-less monument. However, Woodside had become only one hundred acres instead of one thousand acres. It abutted several other coffee and sugar production lands, including Louisiana, St. Thomas, and Morant Bay.

All the estates in Woodside proper and the greater Woodside depended on enslaved labor and indentured servants from Africa. In Brodber's later article "The Bagnolds District of St. Mary, Jamaica, and the Atlantic Crossings of the Late Eighteenth Century," published in 2009, she discusses a little-known phenomenon in the social history of the Greater Woodside area (or the Bagnolds District) of St. Mary. She explores the migration of British Loyalists and enslaved workers from the southern colonies in America to Jamaica before the American Revolution. With the loss of the British in the American Revolution, many of the Loyalists still faithful to Great Britain needed to leave America or be banished, and some went to Jamaica, along with their enslaved persons. Some of these people were among the founding families of Woodside. Brodber indicates that there is a general record of emigration and immigration between Jamaica and the United States and an exchange of culture in terms of music, folklore, art, and writing.[25]

Brodber's discussion of slavery and emancipation is a major subject of her histories and fiction. As she points out in *Woodside, Pear Tree Grove P.O.* and *The Second Generation of Freemen in Jamaica*, the British Parliament passed an act for the abolition of slavery throughout the British colonies on August 1, 1834. However, formerly enslaved persons in Jamaica were first made apprentices before they were freed absolutely. They were to work for their former owners for forty-one and a half hours a week to obtain food, clothing, medicine, and housing. They would exercise freedom during the rest of the time to work for whomever they wished for wages. The system of enslaved labor came to an official end on August 1, 1838, with the British Parliament's passing of the Slavery Abolition Act, when Great Britain declared that all enslaved persons in all its colonies were free.[26]

Both the dates 1834, when the act was passed, and 1838, when full emancipation took effect in the colonies, are alluded to in Brodber's *The Rainmaker's Mistake*, her fourth work of fiction. The novel is speculative fiction about the emancipation of enslaved persons in Jamaica and the difficulty they and slaveholders had in finding work.[27] The newly freed persons, many of whom thought they had been born as yams from Mr. Charlie's land, were faced with learning the truths of all the lies they had been told. They also had to find land to develop for themselves and to form communities and government. They moved to various parts of the land, and some of them shifted to other parts of the continent, including the United States and Canada, and to various aspects of time—past, present, and future.

The many layers of narrative and the multivocal narrative of *The Rainmaker's Mistake* make the novel a different genre of narrative, with a new sense of time. Literary scholar Marie Sairsingh calls this sense of time "recovery of the timeless ancestral bond" that precedes New World existence and "has always existed between Africans and the spirit world."[28] While Sairsingh describes the sense of African spirit and timelessness in *The Rainmaker's Mistake*, the sense of timelessness is also present in other Brodber novels, such as *Myal* and *Nothing's Mat*.

In the history *Woodside, Pear Tree Grove P.O.*, Brodber writes that before slavery ended, there was a camaraderie among the estates of greater Woodside. The production of coffee, sugar, and bananas was very profitable, and products were bought and sold with other parts of Jamaica and the world. There was also much travel among Britain, Jamaica, the United States, and other parts of the world. The religious, governmental, and social worlds worked together. However, with the end of enslaved labor, the world of Woodside turned upside down: "Like an anthill when it is opened or a boil when lanced, this labour erupted with emancipation into individual human beings, each guided by his or her own concerns."[29]

Following emancipation, freedmen found it difficult to acquire land. Much of the land was already owned by British proprietors. House-building material was very costly and was taxed to cut down on the buying of property and building of homes. However, formerly enslaved persons sometimes managed to acquire lands on estates in greater Woodside where they were once enslaved. Small settlements were developed next to the estates where they had worked while enslaved. Formerly enslaved persons who could not buy land might become wage laborers living in barracks. Some obtained responsible jobs with former slaveholders. Brodber notes that a freedman, Quamin Ferguson, even had a child with one of the Neilson daughters, the original owners.[30] There were other such biracial marriages between formerly enslaved persons and Asian Indians who came to the Woodside area as well.

In addition to *Woodside, Pear Tree Grove P.O.*, the sisters discuss several different faiths in their novels and poetry. In Brodber's second novel, *Myal*, the syncretic religion is the titled theme. However, Obeah, which is practiced by the antagonist of the novel, Mass Levi (the old man who wants rejuvenation from the young woman, Anita), is a conflicting force. Obeah is the spiritual force used by Aunt Becca in *Jane and Louisa* to pay for her sins by taking the death of the young man Lester. Also, the Baptist minister, Reverend Simpson, one of the old spirits of the team who appear regularly in *Myal*, and Maydene Brassington, wife of the Methodist minister and daughter of an Anglican priest in England, show that the orthodox Christian denominations were very prominent in the Jamaican rural society portrayed in the sisters' fiction. In Brodber's *Louisiana*, it is hard to imagine any other religion but voodoo (or hoodoo) when thinking of New Orleans and Madame Marie in the Treme District. There the protagonist, Ella Townsend, comes of age and takes on the spirits of the dead Mammy and Lowly Girl, her informants and friends, and enters the minds of the people who come to her for guidance.

In *Woodside, Pear Tree Grove P.O.*, Brodber discusses the lives of free men who followed the first generation of free persons to show how their freedom still confronted many challenges after emancipation. These challenges included acts of God—hurricanes, earthquakes, heavy floods, droughts, and epidemics. Woodside grew more diverse in the late nineteenth century. More Asian Indian, Lebanese, and Chinese shopkeepers and landholders settled the land. The Chinese were less integrated into the culture, and hostilities led to anti-Chinese attacks. More formerly enslaved persons became proprietors, and more laborers were needed to work in the growing estates. There was little land for the second generation of African Jamaicans to purchase because the best land had been bought or was credited to white proprietors. Nevertheless, African Jamaicans continued to build up their agricultural concerns.

Nevertheless, even at the beginning of the twentieth century, the colonial authorities wanted Black people to do physical tasks and to continue toiling on the large estates and dwelling as squatters on the land. Many in the rural areas worked in agriculture on the estates or worked with lumber, shingles, and dyes, burning them for coal, white lime, and firewood. In the cities, they worked as higglers or started haggler shops or were full-time artisans, dressmakers, tailors, shoemakers, launderers, and vendors. A few served in the government in Kingston. A small number of Black Jamaicans became teachers (although public education in Jamaica at the time went only to age fourteen, and then students needed to pay to enter private schools or teacher training colleges). After the earthquake of 1907 and the hurricane of 1917, young people leaned more toward migration than farming or a trade. Many moved to Cuba, Panama, and Canada as a source of cash and employment, and a smaller number went to the United States.

Along with allusions to the Boer Wars, both Brodber and Pollard often refer to Jamaican workers' attraction to the Panama Canal during its construction. The myth of the "Colon Man" (Panamanian) was very appealing to Afro-Jamaicans who were not able to acquire land or jobs in their homeland. The United Fruit Company also employed numerous workers from Jamaica. As a part of the historical context of their novels and poetry, the company provides the basis for cultural connections across the diaspora and the understanding of how class and race jointly span the world.

Both Brodber and Pollard often refer to the involvement of Woodside men in not only the construction of the Panama Canal but also the British military in the Boer Wars. Corpie, the sisters' maternal grandfather, is a recurring character, often mentioned but not usually present in their writings. According to Pollard, he died when her mother was nine years of age, hence his physical absence.[31] Corpie brought back from the war many stories of life in Africa to his family and shared his knowledge of how poorly Black people were treated all over the world due to the impact of slavery and colonialism.

The story of Marcus Garvey, along with his importance to the people of Jamaica and Black people around the world, is essential to many of Brodber's and Pollard's writings. Brodber indicates in her historical writings that many Black people were attracted to Garvey, who was born in St. Ann's Parish in Jamaica and founded his Universal Negro Improvement Association (UNIA) in Jamaica in 1914. His vision of uniting the Black people of the world, creating a government of its own in Africa, and establishing the economic institution of a shipping line engaged Black people in Jamaica and all over the world, with the plan to establish a Black world structure. With Garvey's arrest in the United States and deportation to Jamaica, the failure of his shipping line, and his decision to leave for Great Britain in 1935, there was a less effective organization for change, which led to more strikes of workers in the coal industry, longshoremen on the wharfs, boatmen, and banana loaders. After the 1938 strikes throughout the island, an island-wide land settlement was announced, and Alexander Bustamante, labor leader, founded Jamaica's Labour Party in 1943, became the first prime minister in 1962, and was a cultural hero of the nation.

Garvey, another one of Jamaica's national cultural heroes, looms large in Brodber's and Pollard's work. His words "Look to Africa for the crowning of a Black King, he shall be the Redeemer" seemed to point toward the crowning of Emperor Haile Selassie in Ethiopia in 1930. The emperor was taken to be the divine being that Garvey envisioned, and his reign was a major movement in the development of the Rastafarian movement in Jamaica and around the world in the 1930s. Brodber's interest in Garvey is vital to her lifelong interest in what she calls "the continent of black consciousness," which is both historical and spiritually sustaining to her.

Brodber's third novel, Louisiana, clearly shows the impact of Garvey, his ideas, and the UNIA on all the major characters, particularly Sue Anna Grant-King (Mammy), her husband (Silas King), and her friend Louisa (Lowly Girl). The characters and their family members, Mammy's mother, Ramrod, and other characters were either Garveyites or believers in the idea of resistance, even if it led to their own deaths. Baba in Brodber's first novel, Jane and Louisa Will Soon Come Home, who is Nellie's rescuer in her days of intellectual quandary and confusion, appears to be a Rasta man who teaches her the way to find redemption.

The island of Jamaica finally received its independence from Great Britain in 1962, and colonialism ended. The nation entered the period of neocolonialism and eventually postcolonialism. These socioeconomic conditions seriously hindered the fledgling country and formed some of the context for the sisters' literature. Pollard and

Brodber experienced how the great promise of independence seemed to dim due to the extensive adversity in Jamaica.

Despite her travels around the world and particularly to the United States and other parts of the Caribbean, Brodber has spent most of her time in Woodside. In 1985, she decided to teach community development "with its central motif the giving of information concerning themselves to the people of the community" in her village.[32] Her teaching sessions are held at her home, which has become known as Blackspace. These sessions remain open to the community people and students from various parts of the world who would like to study the people of Woodside, often their ancestors, and their mores to learn more about the culture and ethnicity of Blackness or the African diaspora. In *Woodside, Pear Tree Grove P.O.*, Brodber explains that Blackspace "will be the beginning of self-inquiry into the connection between Jamaica, the villages in and families of Jamaica, the various other places from which Jamaicans were brought to live and work" (vii). The Blackspace "reasonings" begin with a celebration of Emancipation Day, which first took place on August 1, 1962.

In an interview with Keshia Abraham, Brodber speaks to the mission of the Blackspace sessions:

KA: What is the relationship between Blackspace and Woodside? **EB:** That is a relationship I am in the process of working out. For me, Blackspace is for the descendants of enslaved Africans. I think that there is a lot we need to talk about, and I think we should stand up and look at things through our perspective. I don't think that has been done because we're rather embarrassed to have a perspective, or we feel that we don't have a perspective because people tell us all the time that we don't, or people behave as if we don't. But I can't push that onto other people, so my house here and my place around here, what I do inside here, is Blackspace. And Blackspace cooperates with Woodside by supporting the community's educational projects.[33]

In an interview with Catherine John, Brodber discusses how she and her students attempt to recover the lost history of Woodside

Daddy Rock with crowd. Velma Pollard, photographer, 2005. Courtesy of the Pollard Family.

and the various parts of rural Jamaica, the historical relics, and the spiritual and social traditions that have helped them to survive slavery, colonialism, and economic and natural disasters. They have made some of the folklore scribal by writing such books as *My Jamaican Village*, have performed plays about emancipation and independence, and have rescued historical relics. As Brodber explains:

> Historical relics, like the fact that the [Anglican] church in Woodside was the old plantation great house [from the days when the community was a coffee estate]. The steps beside the great house date back to and were made by the Taino. There are places where the enslaved African people on the plantation met to talk to each other in secret [like the cave area called "Daddy Rock"]. There are also Taino sacred places like "One Bubby Susan," and a [lesser known] place called "Sacred Ground," where village people used to have their meetings. The village was also a Convince cult area.[34]

Pollard uses several genres—novels, short stories, nonfiction, and poetry—to write about family, personal relationships, historical events, and places other than Woodside and Jamaica. Like her sister, she writes about her grandmother and mother. The first poem in her first collection of poetry, *Crown Point*, is the title poem about her grandmother. In the poem, the speaker describes her grandmother's home as always being full of "penny-royal smells"—khus-khus from the cupboard and cakes from the oven. Her Bible is open, and she is praying. The speaker even hears her prayers in Trinidad when she lives there. However, her grandmother's voice is not exactly clear: "Perhaps her mystic to me waits my tomorrow's spaces." "Tomorrow's spaces" is a term that Pollard repeatedly uses in her poetry and fiction, apparently referring to the speaker's children or Jamaica's next generation.[35] Through this term, Pollard looks toward the future.

Pollard's poem "Our Mother," also in the collection *Crown Point*, conveys a portrait of a Caribbean woman who is probably familiar to the reader of both sisters' works. She loves to sing, read, and recite poetry. In "Our Mother," dedicated to Pollard's sister, "For Lizzie," the mother is in her coffin. Although it is sunset, the mother is still remembered as full of life: "Orange and red for our mother / Who sang in bright songs . . . / Jigging from side to side / Pointing her index fingers doing the Bustamante."[36]

The major premise of this study is that Erna Brodber and Velma Pollard both present, in their various styles of writing, vivid expressions of Caribbean life with their homeland in rural Jamaica as the central lens. In their writings, they bring to life the language, folklore, religious culture, and history of the place from the period of slavery through the independence of Jamaica and other Caribbean countries.

This book will unfold in the following six chapters. Chapter 2 addresses Pollard's *Karl* and Brodber's *Jane and Louisa Will Soon Come Home*, both of which take place primarily during the 1970s in Jamaica. Chapter 3 examines Brodber's second and third novels, *Myal* and *Louisiana*, and the concepts of spirit possession and spirit theft that they explore. Chapter 4 focuses on Pollard's work, especially her novel *Homestretch* and her five collections of poetry. Chapter 5 examines Brodber's speculative and Afrofuturistic fiction, focusing on her novels *The Rainmaker's Mistake* and *Nothing's Mat* and their themes of time- and space-shifting. Chapter 6 explores the ways Pollard's and Brodber's short fiction portrays the struggles of Jamaican women against a patriarchal society and searches for their own identities. The concluding chapter sums up the book and explains my interest in the sisters' work.

Chapter 2

VELMA POLLARD'S *KARL* AND ERNA BRODBER'S *JANE AND LOUISA WILL SOON COME HOME*

Velma Pollard's first novella was *Karl* (1992), and Erna Brodber's first novel was *Jane and Louisa Will Soon Come Home* (1980). Both take place in the 1960s and 1970s in Jamaica and express the culture and life of the African diaspora. The narrative time of both novels is the years of post-independence when Rastafarianism and reggae were in their heyday and the nation's intelligentsia were consumed with the question of what the newly independent nation would be. Would it be largely influenced by Communist Cuba under the revolutionary Fidel Castro, or would it continue to be democratic and capitalist despite its great debt to the International Monetary Fund (IMF), an international organization that works with nations to stabilize their economies? The IMF is especially important to indebted countries like Jamaica.[1]

As Brian Meeks reports, Prime Minister Michael Manley, who was representative of the People's Nationalist Party (PNP), brought much hope to some nations because of the possibilities of change, but brought terror to others because of fear that the country would become a socialist dictatorship like Cuba.[2] Also according to Meeks, the administration of Manley, Jamaica's fourth prime minister, moved to the left for reform of Jamaica in terms of education, housing, and raising the minimum wage of workers. Manley also began to work more closely with Cuba, to accept Jamaica's debts as declared by the IMF, and to embrace the popular Jamaican music of reggae (the music of Bob Marley) and the concepts of Rastafarians.[3]

Independence was an exciting time in the development of the Rastafari and reggae music. The 1960s and 1970s were also the time of the civil rights and Black Power movements in the United States.

Erna Brodber in the garden in Woodside. Private Collection of Velma Pollard. Courtesy of the Pollard Family.

Rastafari began in Jamaica in the 1930s; however, after Haile Selassie, the emperor of Ethiopia, visited Jamaica in 1966, Rastafarians settled on the idea that he was a god that they would follow, and their doctrine for independence would emulate the early Pan-Africanism of the Jamaican hero Marcus Garvey.[4] After independence, images of the Rastafari and the music and songs of reggae in the voices of such groups as Toots and the Maytals, Toots Hibbert, and Bob Marley and the Wailers brought ideas and symbolism from African folklore and Rastafarian thought to the foreground in the world and in the thought and election of leaders in Jamaica.[5] Rastafarian thought resounds in the language and fiction of Erna Brodber and Velma Pollard in their early works.

EXPLORATIONS OF NEOCOLONIALISM, RASTAFARIANISM, AND LANGUAGE IN POLLARD'S *KARL*

Pollard's first work of longer fiction, *Karl*, a novella, was first published bilingually by Casa de las Americas in Spanish and English in 1992, at which time she won the Casa de las Americas Prize for Literature.[6]

Pollard's narrative technique is more linear than Brodber's. Pollard's narratives generally move through real-world space and time; on the other hand, Brodber uses waves of thought in her narratives, and the waves may occur across time and space, even from the living to the dead. However, *Karl* and *Jane and Louisa* have certain ideas and strategies in common. Both narratives are, in part, bildungsroman in which the protagonists grow up and leave home to go to universities in other countries, including Canada and the United States.[7] Both are filled with the protagonists' expectations of developing themselves as intelligent, quick-witted Jamaican students who are also haunted by the dangers of coming into maturity and having to make sexual choices. Both protagonists suffer certain concurrent disappointments before returning home. The characters in the two works are also forced to face the demands of a nation moving swiftly into its independence from colonial control and toward new possibilities.

In his early life in rural Jamaica, Karl sees himself as the nephew of Aunti and the grandson of Gramps. He is happy, even though he never sees his father and later understands that Aunti is acting as both his mother and father since his birth father, Boy-Boy, had walked away. However, he loves to hear about his grandfather's travels to the Panama Canal, where he stayed until he became unhealthy and was forced to return home.[8] References to the important resource that the building of the Panama Canal became for Jamaican workers between 1904 and 1914[9] are made by both Pollard and Brodber in many of their books. In *Karl*, the building of the canal provided much of the money that Karl's grandfather made for the building of his house and indirectly for the care of his daughter, Aunti, and his grandson, Karl. Besides the money that the Panama Canal provided for Gramps, it also is a source of pride for Karl, who is happy that his grandfather had traveled and taken part in such an important venture. Aunti looks out for Gramps and keeps his house, although it takes a great deal of penny-pinching. Gramps is also a major supporter of the young Karl, whose prizes in school lead him to win a scholarship and continue to study in high school and then in a Canadian university.

Karl understands his low point in the class structure of neocolonial Jamaica, however, when Pearl, a young woman at the university whom he thought he would marry, stops dating him when she realizes that

Aunti works in the market and is really Karl's mother and not married to his father. Pearl's mother does not approve. Even his grandfather's work on the Panama Canal was questionable. Karl has an epiphany: "What could I ever be to her indeed, stripped of all my class prizes and scholarships; Karl, son of Aunti; grandson of Gramps, and short and black besides." Pearl and Karl "were from two different Jamaicas."[10]

Instead of Pearl, Karl marries Daphne, a girl he had known at Peter's Hall, a Jamaican high school. He was a pupil-teacher in Jamaica, and she did not like him then because he wrote her name on the blackboard for talking in class.[11] Daphne had studied nursing in England and gone to Canada, where she became one of the "6-month-night duty" nurses. Black nurses were imported "since white nurses were running from those shifts."[12] At this time when reggae was popularized worldwide by Bob Marley and the Rastafarians,[13] Karl and Daphne run into each other at a dancehall in Waterloo, Canada, and they dance all the latest dances—mento, ska, bop-stop, meringue, chacha. The narrator gives a clear sense of the music of the time and conveys an understanding that the attraction between Karl and Daphne is physical, not emotional or intellectual. Nevertheless, they marry and return to Jamaica, but to the capital city of Kingston, not to Karl's home in Hopeville, in the rural area. Hopeville sounds much like the village of Hopewell, which was adjacent to Woodside.[14]

Karl takes a job in a prosperous bank, Fenton-Smith, in Kingston. Daphne loves living there, but she talks too much at business parties and almost gets him fired. She loves the social life and becomes part of it more than he does. He wants to have children, but she does not want to lose her shape. Karl's mother, Aunti, thinks, "Miss Daph a little extra . . . a little too cris" [Jamaica Creole for pretentious].[15] Pollard brings in the title of her third book of poetry, *The Best Philosophers I Know Can't Read or Write* (2004), and her sister's *Jane and Louisa* in reference to the unhappy marriage of Karl and Daphne. Karl tells Daphne that one little old man used to say, "If you love the man you have, you will love the child you have. . . . That must mean you will take the trouble to have the child. Our land is full of roadside philosophers."[16]

Daphne joins all kinds of women's society groups but rejects Karl's dreams. Karl thinks, "I never asked her into my garden, beautiful or not beautiful, so now I can't expect her to help me pick out the weeds."[17] Daphne sometimes wants to pick up Karl in the car after his work, but she has ladies' club meetings to attend. "Wait on the house; change the car; then wait on Daphne," Karl thinks.[18] Karl wants to be an active father, as his father, Boy-Boy, was not. His mother, Aunti, had finally told Karl about her disappointment in his father when the son was nearly nineteen: "And when I saw the shame and grief and loneliness in her, and the tears welling up, I just hugged her and told her not to cry. I didn't bother to tell her how many years I had known. Nobody believes they drop out of hollow wood; at least not for very long."[19]

In *Karl*, the male protagonist loses his self-confidence and his mind, while his wife prospers in the social world into which she is projected. This book portrays class and color within the Afro-Jamaican world; in other words, it is about neocolonialism as well as Rastafarian voice. A voice of change, the Rastafarian voice, speaks throughout the story as a constant reminder to Karl that he is entering too much into the world of Babylon, the materialistic world that the Rastafarians consider the enemy. The voice of Jamaican folklore, so much a part of Brodber's literary world, is also heard often in *Karl*. Pollard describes the novel on its title page as a "monologue . . . in the mind of . . . a man!!!!"[20] The first chapter of the book seems to be from the mind of Karl after he has lost his mind and is in a mental institution. He says rhythmically in Jamaica Creole:

> Im is a self-made man
> Im mek imself
> Das why im no mek good.[21]

Pollard shows her major interest in language in this writing, as she does in her book *Dread Talk: The Language of the Rastafari* (1994). Karl is a well-educated man, and as a boy and young man, he had great aptitude in school, won many prizes, and handled Standard Jamaican English very well. However, after his time in Canada and higher education training, he speaks to the Rasta Man and uses Jamaica Creole English, while the Rasta Man who ventures into the narrative on several occasions uses Dread Talk or Rasta language, which Pollard defines as "a comparatively recent adjustment of the lexicon of Jamaica Creole to reflect the religious, political and philosophical positions of the believers in Rastafari."[22] In *Dread Talk*, Pollard discusses the language that has evolved out of the movement of Rastafari. In its epigraph, she quotes the poem "Mabrak" by Bongo Jerry, a noted Rastafarian poet: "Mabrak is righting the wrongs and brain-whitening—HOW? / Not just by washing out the straightening and wearing / dashiki t'ing. / MOSTOFTHESTRAIGHTENINGISINTHETONGUE— SO HOW?"[23]

As Eric Doumerc (author of *Caribbean Civilization*, teacher, and researcher specializing in Caribbean poetry, music, and oral tradition) has noted, Bongo Jerry's poem defamiliarizes the poetry by omitting spacing in the lines; it shows that language has power and "creates a new reality."[24] That impact was the power of Rastafarian, or dub, poetry. In *Karl*, both the businessman of Babylon (Karl) and the Rasta Man are parts of Karl's mind. His "monologue in the mind of a man," the subtitle of the novella's original title, is a dialogue between Karl and his other self. Pollard points out that the poet Mervyn Morris, poet and professor emeritus at the University of the West Indies at Mona, has defined the term "Mabrak" as "a Rastafarian concept meaning 'black lightning.'"[25]

Karl's Aunti does not even see the Rasta Man, also known as Rasta I; he is beyond her purview. As the narrator notes, when Karl left his home with Aunti in the rural area of Hopeville, near Woodside, he would encounter Rasta I "with his multicolored tam and pointed beard . . . a prophet" in Kingston, where he attended private school after Aunti raised money through much persistence and determination by making and selling an endless number of pies. Rasta I would say rhythmically to Karl:

"Y'ou gwine to Babylon school man!"

"Mmmhmmmmmm."

"Noh she mi nevva warn you."

"Mmmmhmmmmmmm."

"Oh Babyloooooooooooon, why dost thou despoil my children? Their feet shall seek no more the temples of the wicked. . . . Soon! Soooon!"[26]

Rasta I is a city man whose ideas are Rastafarian, but he cannot be heard by many in the rural areas who believe in education and participation in the newly independent government, not the culture of Rastafarians, which was associated with drugs, squatting on the land, and using others' property to grow marijuana and other crops.[27]

Karl suffers a nervous breakdown after working for several years at Fenton-Smith Bank in Kingston and must enter a hospital for his mental condition. As a matter of fact, the novella begins with Karl in the mental institution hearing the "tip, tip, tip of a recurrent drop of water . . . sending a slow, pure, stream of calm through a narrow, endless hole [that] pierced through the chaos in Karl's head."[28] After learning that Karl and his wife are no longer happy together, the reader discovers that one Sunday at the Hopeville church service Karl had looked out of the church window at the path that runs past the church and by the graveyard. He felt the need to walk down the path to find peace, as his old girlfriend, Pearl, used to search for such places in the countryside to be alone when she returned to Jamaica to teach. Karl finds it hard to find these times of silence, and this absence is one of the things that makes him feel shell-shocked like Mr. Rinyon, his neighbor in Woodville, who never got over World War II and drank porter wine endlessly, and like another neighbor, Maas Clifton, who was very bright in school but had studied too hard or had succumbed to an obeah attack. Karl thinks, "Draft porter, shell shock: Clifton, duppy shock, or book shock; Karl . . . life shock. What a mess!!!"[29]

People like Aunti (Karl's birth mother) and her father (Gramps) look up to education and prosperity, as Velma Pollard and Erna Brodber's parents and relatives did. The characters in the novel, as well as most members of the middle class in Jamaica, thought that Rastafarians were throwing away their opportunities and believing in a dream world. Karl's experiences in the mental institution are not clear, but the narrator continues Karl's monologue and conversation with Rasta I. He considers that moving from the simple, poor life in Hopeville to life as a corporate employee or partner in Kingston was not easy. He finds it impossible to leave the recreational world of cricket and dominoes to go into the world of golf and polo, thinking, "Somewhere between church and golf is a whole generation of us fighting, looking, and not finding . . . like you walking through a swamp and the mangrove roots tying up your foot."[30] He remembers the people who had tried to move up in class in Hopeville and how Aunti and Gramps had laughed when those people made fools of themselves.

Karl tells the hospital attendant that he is scheduled to leave the mental institution the next day, but he recalls a dream when he tried to enter his home on the hill and could not do it; he had to go back down the hill. After hearing Karl's story, "'Boss,' says the hospital attendant, 'It look like you get to like this place you know. You sure you can go back to Babylon?'"[31] He is not ready. When Teacher Brown comes to see him, he is still not ready. He will not leave the hospital. He dreams of Aunti looking through the nail hole in his head and crying. He has gone through his own crucifixion and cannot move. Daphne is sad but understands in her own way.

In the Epilogue, ten years after Karl dies, a young man named Kenneth visits his teacher, "an old, black man; tall, stately, with a face from the mold of the Lion of Judah—lanky jaws, thin nose, unsplayed nostrils and pointed chin"; sitting in his rocking chair on the porch, he looks like Emperor Haile Selassie, Ras Tafari, who was considered by the Rastafarians to be divine or the Messiah.[32] Nevertheless, a new time had dawned in the millennium. Wearing a tam and beard, suggesting a revolutionary, Kenneth tells Teacher that he has not attempted to go the way of the younger "Bright Boys" like Karl. Kenneth has started his own small business. He continues, "You have to find out what you want and take it you know. . . . Babylon can only hold you as strong as you allow it."[33] Babylon, an important symbol throughout the novel, was considered by the Rastafarians to be Black people's opponent. Teacher cries when he thinks about Karl and how he had been strangled by Babylon.

The novel ends with Teacher thinking that Karl's time has ended, and a more peaceful, tolerant period has begun. The narrator ends *Karl* with "Truly, the Keeper of Israel has not slept." The words repeat the ideas of Psalms 121:4–6: "Behold, he that keepeth Israel shall neither slumber nor sleep. The Lord is thy keeper; the Lord is thy shade upon thy right hand."[34] The Rastafarians speak of themselves as Israel, and they believe the Second Coming is at hand. Velma Pollard predicted the coming acceptance of Rastafarian beliefs. Anglican Church hymnals in the twenty-first century are adding songs by reggae legends Bob Marley, Peter Tosh, and others because of their belief in redemption and transformation, and Rastafarian beliefs have spread to England and Europe, the United States, Canada, Africa, Australia, and New Zealand.[35]

In *Karl*, post-independence Jamaica has moved forward into new conceptions of itself as a nation in which young people can develop their own businesses, and the government has encouraged such production and creativity. However, Karl could not move into the new age; he died in a mental institution. Jamaica, at the time of the novel, was not ready either. It needed to fight against its indebtedness and to deal with a reluctant Western world and many Jamaicans who opposed the style and ideas of Prime Minister Michael Manley, who seemed too close to the world of Cuba and dictatorship.

JAMAICAN AND PERSONAL INDEPENDENCE IN BRODBER'S *JANE AND LOUISA WILL SOON COME HOME*

In Brodber's *Jane and Louisa Will Soon Come Home*, there is an interplay between the characters' personal independence and Jamaican independence. The characters' growth is an allegory or metaphor for the growing up of the country of Jamaica in the first decade after its independence in 1962 and its election of the forward-looking Prime Minister Manley in 1972. The country was attempting to claim its own identity, language, music, and culture.[36] After finding herself lost in the intellectual ponderings of the time in her meetings with other young radicals, Nellie, the novel's protagonist, is saved by her old friend and spiritual healer, Baba, a Myalist, and her great-aunt Alice, who has already undergone her translation into the other world as an ancestor who is always there for the family of succeeding generations.

The narrator of *Jane and Louisa* describes a *kumbla* as being "like a beach ball. It bounces with the sea but never goes down."[37] The narrator also compares the *kumbla* to "an eggshell that does not crack, a seamless calabash, a parachute, and a comic strip space ship" that

you can see into and out of; it is a "safe, protective time capsule."[38]
It was possible for Nellie to hide in her village, "a mossy covert that
did not even have a finger post man."[39] The village of Woodside in
St. Mary Parish was a secret for the most part, at least until Mass Mehiah
built a new fundamentalist church there and young girls grew up and
found the "snail" or sexual knowledge. Nellie hears many stories about
the snail before she enters puberty. After all, she did sleep at the foot
of her mother and father's bed in her early days and, no doubt, heard
rumblings as they conceived six children. Among the voices that the
narrator shares with the reader in the first chapter, we hear someone,
probably Nellie's mother, talking to her lover, Alexander Richmond,
who will become her husband. She says, "Mother says I must stop
writing to you," and the lover responds, "Show her your waist." Granny
Tucker (we assume) says about her daughter Sarah, "The chile life
spoil. Lord take the case. Those sneaking khakhi lips forcing poor
little Baptist contractions."[40] The *kumbla* was a protective device; in
Rhonda Cobham's words, "Nellie's kumbla of respectability saves her
from 'spoiling' herself and ensnares her academic success."[41]

In the early chapters in the section called "Voices," we also hear
Nellie asking her Aunt Becca if she can go to the movies with Baba,
Mass Stanley's nephew, to see *Jack the Ripper*, and Aunt Becca says no
because she must continue to protect Nellie, who was then sixteen:
"Woman luck at a dungle heap, fowl come scratch it up."[42] Aunt Becca
says that her niece must watch herself. Her Cousin B had not done
so and ended up bearing Baba illegitimately.[43] The reader soon finds
out that Aunt Becca had also "fallen" early in life and had terminated
her pregnancy. In payment for her sin, Aunt Becca's cousin Lester had
been sacrificed. As Brodber and Pollard note throughout their writing,
women, especially in the rural areas, have a difficult time living up to
social expectations and still living their natural lives and meeting their
family and artistic and/or employment goals. Brodber writes, "Once a
year Aunt Dorcas sat with us in person. Uncle Lester too occasionally.
He it was who took the death of Aunt Becca. (We know that for Mass
Tanny was confessing.)"[44] We suspect that Lester's death was a case
of the African-inspired spiritual practice of Obeah.[45]

Nellie is only eight years old when Aunt Becca sends her a straw
bag with a beautiful strap decorated with red and green butterflies

that she should wear diagonally across her chest, something that she had always prayed for; she also receives a yellow organdy dress for Easter and another dress for her birthday, on the Saturday before Easter. The plenty embarrasses her so much that she forgets her lines in the Easter cantata: "Aunt Becca, did you send that bag to shame me, to whittle down my world, to stop me from enjoying it," thinks Nellie.[46] The snail is that part of a Caribbean girl's experience that she must come to terms with, even if she is socially damned forever for doing so. When Nellie is eleven years of age, she begins to realize that her male friends stop playing with her in any tumble-down way; her father looks at her very skeptically and says, "Oh my, how you've grown," and her mother tells her that very soon she will have "it" (her menstruation), and she will have to go to her Aunt Becca, the teacher of all such social things and of propriety. Consequently, Nellie goes to live with her aunt, who protects her from boys such as Baba.

Later, when Nellie has gone off to school in "Sam's country" (the United States), she encounters a boy in a dark movie theater and interacts with the snail. She wants to but does not run away from "the mekke thing"; that is, she goes through maturation.[47] Kevin Arthur Cryderman, in his essay "The Language of *Jane and Louisa*," argues that Nellie wanted to stay in her hiding place too long: "The kumbla," he says, "is a cocoon in which metamorphosis occurs; yet it also skirts dangerously close to swallowing one up in fragility if one remains there for too long."[48]

In this her first novel, Brodber weaves together a narrative of the history of family, community, and spirit. The family story begins in the first chapter but is not fully told until one of the last episodes in the last section, called "The Moving Camera." Later we have the final chapters, "The Pill" and "The Fish." By the end of the novel, Nellie has gone through her growing up years, including puberty and life at a university in the United States, and has returned to Jamaica, joining the Rastafari movement and a group of thinkers similar to Lloyd Best, George Beckford, Trevor Monroe, and Norman Girvan.[49] As Roberts points out, Nellie and the thinkers live in a government yard and have regular meetings to discuss the state of the country in the first years of its independence.[50]

Nellie's return home to Woodside leads her to meet her ancestors and discover more about her own identity and that of the community.

Through the spying glass and the moving camera provided by her grandfather's daughter, Alice Whiting, who speaks from the dead, Nellie sees and experiences the lives of her ancestors.[51] According to literary critics Daria Zheltukhina and Evelyn O'Callaghan, Brodber became a member of the Twelve Tribes of the Rastafarians and joined a group of leftist thinkers led by George Beckford, Lloyd Best, Norman Gervan, and others after returning to Jamaica from the United States.[52]

In an interview with Petal Samuel, Brodber discussed her experiences with such groups. Brodber says, "Sometime in the early to late 1960s, there was a kind of move towards *examining* our political beliefs, *examining* our Independence. And there were people at the university [now the University of the West Indies in Mona, Jamaica], such as Lloyd Best and George Beckford, who said, 'Examine your condition. What is this Independence about?'"[53] In *Jane and Louisa*, the names of the historical leaders and planners of the intellectual movement of young people are not identified, but they are significant figures behind the characters.[54]

The narrator repeats the phrase "I came home" throughout the section called "Miniatures." However, during the period that Nellie stays in the government yard, where she regularly has intellectual meetings with her friends Erroll, Barry, and Egbert and serves as secretary, her apparent lover, Robin, dies. In Nellie's words:

> The night my young man got caught up in the spirit and burnt to grease like beef suet caught in a dutchie pot, I wept so hard my tears no longer held salt. Such a frightfully humiliating way to die.... He reminded us of the transfiguration, of how Elijah and Christ became one.[55]

This moment represents what Roberts calls "the ground zero of Nellie's search for identity and salvation from the false *kumblas* offered by her family history."[56] Brodber uses the episode as an allegory for the mental and physical loss of the young Black intellectuals and revolutionaries of the time. Brodber found thinkers who captured her imagination and that of many young people of the Caribbean as they planned the burgeoning changes of their nations after independence.

In her essay "Who Was Cock Robin? A New Reading of Erna Brodber's *Jane and Louisa Will Soon Come Home*," Darryl Dance, who has published many essays about Brodber and Pollard, says that Cock Robin, Nellie's sweetheart, "was really Nellie's alter ego. . . . He didn't really exist—but just represented the black intellectual whose mission was to contribute to the making of the New Jamaica."[57]

Nellie's childhood friend Baba begins to appear at the meetings of the friends in the government housing; she eventually finds that he came to save her. He is a young man from her past, really the grandson of Elsada and Mass Stanley Ruddock, son of their son David, whom they had put out of the house because of his disputes with his father. Baba had been a neighbor and had asked Nellie out to a movie once, but Aunt Becca said no. Now he comes to the meetings of the group of political activists in the government yard and never says a word. He smells of lime and whittles a figure out of pear seeds: first, the head, neck, arms, hip, then legs of a child.

At his seventh meeting, he takes the sculpture to Nellie and lays it on top of her minutes, and the figure of pear seeds crumbles. His point seems to be that Nellie and her compatriots have just been wasting their time discussing ideas of what the new Jamaica should be. In anger, she says, "I would beard that low-down, high-handed outsider in his den and let him have all he'd been asking."[58] However, she goes with him to his very neat apartment and is entranced by his demeanor and his wisdom, recuperates from her mental breakdown, and returns home to Woodside. Nellie begins to come back to herself "with rest, a good diet of soups and eggnog, insulin, and conversations with neighbors in the compound." She begins to feel that she had a purpose, and "it lay through water, through his tears and mine. Wasn't that the lesson? Or was this obeah man of an anancy trying to play something else on me!"[59]

Brodber speaks of both Baba and Aunt Alice as Anancy figures or shamans. They are both healers who interact with the spirit. Baba had once been a childhood friend, smarter and more versatile than most, but she can soon see that he is different. He is more serious than her other friends; he can work with her spiritually and heal her mind and body, causing a transformation within her and making it possible for her to come outside of herself and her *kumbla* and discover her true self and her family's past and present. He heals her, so that she can make herself whole again. Erna Brodber and her sister both use Anancy characters and strategies in many of their novels, stories, and poems.[60] In *Jane and Louisa*, Baba is an agent of transformation, not the usual idea of Anancy as a trickster spirit. He saves Nellie by helping her open her eyes and see into her soul and the past.

Brodber also refers to other Anancy tales in the novel. One of them is the tale of Anancy and Dryhead. Anancy tricks Dryhead into thinking he has several sons that he will leave with him if he allows his son to help him pilot the boat home; since then they will return, he can hold the other sons as hostages. But in the end, we find that Anancy has just tricked Dryhead; he had only his son, Tucuma, who disguised himself into looking like five different sons. Tucuma's disguises were his *kumblas*, but Baba teaches Nellie to get out of her *kumbla* and be herself, without any protection other than the spirit.

When Nellie's recuperation under Baba's care is complete, she steps out of his home and realizes that her relatives are everywhere around her, like flowers and plants, such as Tia Maria, Madame Faith, and the flower "kiss-me-quick." Aunt Alice (now deceased), the sister of her father's mother, introduces her to a new world. At first, it is a world of dance and mento music: "The music of laughter, sighs, ouches of the saxophone, of tramping shifting feet keeps the tempo going, round and up like the steam in a boiling house." Aunt Alice guides her into the garden. She sees everything as through a "spying glass": "I saw . . . the myriad pieces of crystal littered around this base."[61] Baba and Anancy disappear, but the light comes through the banana leaves, and Nellie is secure with her people. Anancy is off in a *kumbla*, but he still has power.

Through a moving camera, as Nellie walks into her beautiful garden after being taken away from the thinkers in the government yard by Baba and healed by him, she sees her oldest known paternal ancestors, Albert and Elizabeth Whiting of her father's family. Their first child—William Alexander—was christened in the year that Victoria ("a baby girl") was crowned queen of England. According to the narrator:

> It was a baby corn light yellow morning when William Alexander was christened. A baby girl [Victoria] had been

crowned Queen. A monarch but a woman. One doubted her wisdom but never her kindliness. A true queen. For all her kind heart, those heathens had got uppity.[62]

William Alexander was the imagined basis for the family's feeling that a *kumbla* surrounded and protected them. The family generally thought that William Alexander was the first of a great dynasty. After all, his father, Albert Whiting, had quickly become "big massa, hirer of labour, lender of money, powerful miller to the little colony of hillside blacks."[63] However, during Queen Victoria's reign, slavery ended in the British Commonwealth countries, and things became harder for William Alexander's family, which had failed financially.[64]

William Alexander, who was thought to have been the reason for the *kumbla* identity of the family and was the oldest of the ten children of Albert and Elizabeth Whiting, depended totally on the "blue-black nanny," Faith, who took care of him and his siblings when the mother and father died in the children's early lives. Faith could not help it, we are told, when William Alexander fell in love with her "goddy" (godchild), the Black Tia Maria. William Alexander and Tia Maria had a fruitful marriage, and William looked out for his siblings as well as his children. In the meantime, Queen Victoria was getting old, and the Morant Bay Rebellion in Jamaica took place.[65] The juxtaposition of details about Queen Victoria and stories of the Whiting family is an example of Brodber's narrative style and her love of history. As Roberts points out, Brodber uses such surprising turns of thought to satirize and give context to the actions occurring in the Alexander family by describing the simultaneous lives of protagonists of the novel and Queen Victoria.[66]

William Alexander's wife, the Black Tia Maria, "started to weave one of those purely spun *kumblas*, growing out of the top of her head and billowing under her feet somewhat like a bridal ensemble" for each of her children.[67] They all knew the story of their white great-grandfather (William Alexander), but Tia Maria, an embarrassment to herself because of her Blackness, tried to erase herself from the family. Tia Maria's daughter Kitty (Nellie's paternal grandmother) rebelled and married a Black sawyer, a *pattoo* as the narrator calls him derisively. Tia Maria thought this action was a disgrace to the family; she disowned her daughter, left William Alexander to marry another man, and went mad. William Alexander, the source of the *kumbla* identity, found nothing wrong with the Black man that Kitty married: Puppa Richmond, Nellie's paternal grandfather. However, without the help of Tia Maria, William Alexander lost his business. His sister, Nellie's great aunt, Alice, dies but remains in the family to bring advice and solace to the generations to come. Nevertheless, "Great grandfather Will was romance" and remained the foundational metaphor of the family.[68]

In getting to know her family ancestors from their earliest days in Jamaica, Nellie begins to understand why she has fears and uncertainties about her own identity. She also begins to understand why the newly independent Jamaica has its doubts. In the garden to which Aunt Alice takes Nellie first, she feels a part of a watering hole, and she "was a rubber tube floating evenly, deeply, falling through layers of the atmosphere, cool and mossy, no cobwebs. Just cool and mossy. Falling evenly, evenly, at six-foot catchments."[69] Her ancestors come out of the rocks in the garden: "Then seeing the stalagmites and stalagmites turned into people. Like one-bubby Susan rising out of her graven image."[70] She hears her mother's mezzo-soprano voice and sees her father and Puppa (Richmond, the *pattoo*), her father's father, then her other relatives, including Granny Tucker and Corpie, her great-grandfather William Alexander (who was nearly white), and Tia Maria, the thin Black woman who married him.

All her family members take shapes and colors in a musical production.[71] In it, she is a part of a dance performance, similar to those in which she used to participate with Stanley Ruddock, Baba's grandfather, in the old days. The family and community are trying to communicate with her. They sing "banana mullum"; her mother sings an aria in her clear voice from Nellie's childhood. They all welcome her there. Tia Maria beats the kettle drum, and someone plays the bamboo sax. They play the whole reel and wait for her questions and answers. All her kin are there, and she sits in her granny's parlor. They all sing, "We did our part. Blessings on yours."[72] She wants to ask questions, but they have left, and she is left perspiring and feeling "those funny stripes on my behind."[73] They are the stripes of the spying glass through which Aunt Alice showed her the people and the performance. Aunt Alice continues: "Wake up Nellie. She tried. It's your time now and I can take you no further."[74] Then Aunt Alice takes her moving camera and assures Nellie that "Jane and Louisa will soon come home."[75]

Many members of the family tell Nellie she must come out of the *kumbla* and do her part in making a new productive life for the community. She has seen many of her cousins fall, but she has also heard her granny using her strong, "wiry black hands" and praying and reminded them that they must keep their heads up high and use their hands. Nellie dreams that she is carrying a fish, but has much trouble bearing it. Nevertheless, she still feels that "It will come."[76] The birth of the fish seems to be Nellie's own birth or becoming. However, it is also the birth of the newly independent Jamaica. What will it be like? Will it be truly independent? Will it be economically strong and independent from the colonial powers that have attempted to determine its leaders? She hasn't come into a full understanding of herself and her relationship with her family and community yet, or the nation's true development, but the fruition will come. Jane and Louisa will soon come home. "We are getting ready," the book ends.[77]

In Pollard's novella, Karl is tormented by the Rastafarian spirit of the 1960s and 1970s because he is confused about what his mission should be. Should he seek wealth and prosperity and accept the Babylonian goals, or should he seek redemption and develop himself spiritually? He cannot continue with his material dreams and collapses mentally, never to return to sanity. Similarly, Nellie in Brodner's *Jane and Louisa* is also confused and loses her way until she returns to Jamaica and to her family and community in Woodside. Because of her family and community guides Aunt Alice and Baba, she is brought back to reality and is reintroduced to her ancestors, her community, and her culture.

Chapter 3

SPIRIT THEFT AND SPIRIT POSSESSION IN ERNA BRODBER'S *MYAL* AND *LOUISIANA*

This chapter presents an analysis of Erna Brodber's second and third novels, *Myal* and *Louisiana*, which are studies of the Voodoo concepts of spirit theft and spirit possession. Velma Pollard's writings are seldom addressed in this chapter. Pollard's books such as *Karl* and *Dread Talk* are studies of Rastafari cosmogony, but they are not lived experiences, as are found in Brodber's writings.

Spirit theft is a key concept explored in *Myal*. Spirit theft is the stealing of one's soul or spirit, as discussed in Anne Margaret Castro's "Sounding Out Spirit Thievery in Erna Brodber's 'Myal.'"[1] The two protagonists of *Myal* suffer from spirit thievery. Ella O'Grady suffers because her husband attempts to steal or appropriate her ideas about her homeland. She loses her spirit by what he has done but is eventually saved by people who practice Myal and Kumina (African-derived religious traditions) or by the elder spirits, who were originally from Africa. Anita, the other protagonist, also loses her spirit for a while because an old man, Mass Levi, tries to steal her spirit and sexuality to build up his own. However, Anita is finally saved by the resilience of the African-derived religious traditions. Mass Levi's Obeah does not work in the end.

Spirit possession is a key concept explored in *Louisiana*. Ella Townsend Kohl is a counterpart to Ella O'Grady of *Myal*, although this novel's Ella is more of a leader than the other Ella. She sets out to find out about Black people of southwest Louisiana. But she comes to be possessed by the souls of Mammy and her friend, Lowly Girl. Ella Townsend's soul possession with the women is partially voluntary. After she begins to know more about the other people who share

The sisters together in a classroom. Private Collection of Velma Pollard. Courtesy of the Pollard Family.

their knowledge with her at Madame Marie's boarding house in New Orleans, she begins to know more about herself as well. She also learns that Mammy, her husband, Silas, and her friend Lowly Girl are all Garveyites. They all support Marcus Garvey's decision to go back to Africa, and they spread his teachings through Louisiana, Chicago, where they meet, and Jamaica, where Garvey was born and developed his ideas.

MYAL AND SPIRIT THEFT

In *Myal*, both the protagonists Ella and Anita are subjects of spirit thievery. In the novel, the first protagonist, Ella O'Grady is a biracial child of a Black Jamaican mother, Mary Riley, a native of Grove Town in St. Thomas Parish, and an Irish police officer who works in Grove Town for a while and needs a housekeeper for that time. He rapes Mary, but she refuses to leave her home in rural Jamaica when she becomes pregnant and goes to work in the banana and cane fields with her "alabaster" child in a basket and brings the child up as a single parent. "Mussa think is Moses and Miriam," says the narrator in Jamaica Creole language, as Velma Pollard describes such language in *Dread Talk*.[2]

Brodber also makes frequent references to the Christian Bible. In Exodus 2:9, Moses was taken to the Nile river by his mother in a basket because the Egyptian pharaoh had decreed the killing of all Jewish babies. Moses' sister, Miriam, asked the pharaoh's daughter, who saw the baby in the basket, to keep the baby, and she would send a woman to care for him. The woman was Moses' mother, who cared for him as a baby and young child.

In the first scene of the novel, Mary's grown-up daughter Ella has been brought back to Grove Town after suffering spirit theft by her white American husband, Selwyn Langley, who is a dramatist. When the novel begins, Mass Cyrus, an herbalist and Myalman, is attempting to cure Ella of the terrible illness she has acquired over the time that she was with her husband. The restoration of her soul will take place in seven days of Myal ritual,[3] as the Judeo-Christian creation did.

The novel also tells the story of the other protagonist, Anita, the daughter of another single mother, Euphemie. Anita is an extremely bright fifteen-year-old girl who suffers another type of spirit theft. Teacher Holness, headmaster of the local school, and his wife, Amy, decide to ask her mother if they can take her to protect her from the young men who seem to be attempting to win her over and take her away from her books. Teacher and his wife soon recognize that Anita is in more danger than they thought; in fact, she seems to be subject to the old man, Mass Levi, who is using the occult practice of Obeah to enter her body and possess her spirit in order to strengthen his aged and almost depleted sexual powers. His purpose is a major effort of spirit theft. According to Fernandez-Omos and Paravisini-Gerbert:

> The ritual of the Myal dance, hypnotic dancing in circles under the leader's direction, involved as well a mesmerizing opening the entrance of the spirit in the body of the initiate, providing a bridge between the spirit possession characteristics of Afro-Creole practices and the filling with the Holy Spirit found in some variants of New World Christianity.[4]

The events of spirit theft that attack both Ella and Anita threaten to take away the powers and identity of the two young women. The first theft is the colonialist rewriting of Ella's history that she undergoes in the Jamaican schools and as the wife of the white Selwyn Langley. The second theft is an inside attack on Anita, leaving her as a zombie or husk of her true self and with the old man in possession of her spirit. The Myalist spirits of Grove Town, the village adjacent to Morant Bay, where many believe in Myal, provide the strength to resist and cure both women of their attacks.

The first type of soul theft described in the novel deals with Ella's loss of spirit because of her colonial style of education, which dealt with her cultural background before Jamaica received its independence from Great Britain. Her husband does not accept Ella as a full person in her own right with a strong culture of her own. Although the heir of a long line of chemists, manufacturers of medicines, and doctors, he has moved away from his family business because it bores him.

The novel begins with Ella lying prostrate in the grove of Mass Cyrus, as he works assiduously, with the help and fear of many of the grove's living creatures, to restore the young woman's soul. He looks at the face of this woman cradled in the leaves of "the bastard cedar tree." All the trees, plants, and flowers in his grove shake with grief. Mass Cyrus, the Myalman, stares at the prostrate body of his patient, her face in the cup of his palms, while he listens to the cries in his grove. He thinks, "This pain, confusion, and destruction are what these new people bring to themselves and to this world."[5]

Mass Cyrus, or the ancestral elder spirit that he embodies, who is also known as "Percy the chick," cures Ella and plays the trumpet. As one of the higher spirits in the novel, he is associated with the trumpet.[6] In the description of the rituals that Mass Cyrus uses to cleanse Ella's body of all the spiritual pain, Brodber brings together many of the important themes of the novel, particularly spirit theft and hybridity, the spiritual tradition of Myal, and other religious traditions, such as soul restoration. Ella O'Grady is one of the "new people" of hybrid cultures. Hybridity has become a major concept in postcolonial thought partly because of the many mixed cultures that had become leaders of the world politically, economically, and socially, as in the many religions and cultures described in *Myal*. Hybridity or cultural diversity is an important aspect of the novel and indeed both sisters' writing.[7] From the perspective of Mass Cyrus, these people are too "sekkle pekkle": "they come blasting my ears and shaking my etheric [energy] with their clashing cymbals. This discord could shake a man out of his roots."[8] Ella and her blindness to the world have caused great discord, and the poison in her has grown into a large grey mass, "the stinkiest, dirtiest ball to come out of a body since creation,"[9] which Mass Cyrus is faced with the task of removing. The job frightens all the creatures of his grove and puts the trees into an orgasmic frenzy. All the spirits of Grove Town know that the Myalist, with the help of the trees and creatures and his "etheric," has the power to restore Ella.[10]

Ella had accepted the colonial rhetoric of her education in Grove Town, and she had accepted the host of imaginary characters of her reading, for example, Peter Pan and Daisy Maid. She also loved the map of Europe. Therefore, in her mind, there was no surprise when she was asked to recite Rudyard Kipling's poem "The White Man's Burden" for the school.[11] She never considered that she was not just talking about "you Big Steamers" travelling all over the world—Quebec, Hong Kong, Bombay—but, in fact, she was also describing the European culture's assessment of people like her. Because of her excellent recitation, people start to notice Ella, and she is adopted by the Methodist minister, Rev. William Brassington, and his wife.

Maydene Brassington is also interested in adopting Ella to help her husband accept his heritage, for he was a "white Jamaican," of European and African heritage.[12] Mrs. Brassington asks Teacher's wife, Amy Holness, if she would be willing to ask Ella's mother, Mary, if Maydene can adopt her child:

> "You do know that my husband is Jamaican"—Amy knew she meant "not full white" and at another time would have feigned surprise, [saying,] "But Mrs. Brassington, how extraordinary." Today she was silent and Maydene went on.—"There are things about him that I can't understand. When I saw that child, I saw him."[13]

Brodber is dealing with the theme of "third space" in the fact of Reverend Brassington's hybridity and in this conversation between the two women. Third space and hybridity are Homi Bhabha's terms for cultural change, as in the different ways of speaking and the different manners of understanding of Amy Holness, the teacher's wife, and Maydene Brassington, the British wife of the biracial Methodist minister, Reverend Brassington.[14] The conversation is also an example of what Brodber calls "linguistic ritual."[15]

The two women seldom come out and say what is on their minds, but instead move gingerly around the awkward situation. Mrs. Holness still wonders why Mrs. Brassington wants to "adopt" the child Ella. Was it to have a young woman in her house to be available for her sons' whims when they returned from school in England to visit their parents in Jamaica? And Mrs. Brassington wants to make sure that Mrs. Holness does not ignore what she is trying to say because they are of different races and classes. In the end, Amy Holness decides to help Maydene Brassington because she could be of help to her husband, Teacher, in getting another grade level for his school from the British government and to her own out-of-wedlock son, who could use some help in gaining admission into a training school.[16]

One of the multiple layers of the narration is the story of Ella O'Grady's heritage, which is a story of cultural diversity. Earlier in the narrative, we find out that before Ella's mother, Mary Riley, had gone to Morant Bay at the request of Amy Holness to become the housekeeper of the Irish policeman, she had been raised by her parents, Catherine Riley and Bada D.:

> Bada D. was strangeness itself. The man had thin lips, pointed nose and the hair thick and strong and curly like a coolie royal through [*sic*] Indian was nowhere in his strain for he steps straight off an African boat. That was common knowledge. Call himself a Moor. Said he came from Tanja and he was going back there. Mount Horeb was a hill where the man would sit for hours looking at the St. Thomas Sea and dreaming about flying back to Africa.[17]

Bada D. personifies the diverse population of Jamaican society. In her nonfiction account of her home village, Woodside, Brodber discusses the many different nationalities and ethnic groups—African,

European, American, Chinese, Indian, Lebanese, and Jewish—that immigrated to St. Mary Parish and the surrounding parishes in the nineteenth century. Bada D., Ella's maternal grandfather, also practiced the African-inspired religion of Kumina. He was a strong person in the family, but so was Ella's mother, who helped her husband with the farming until she grew weak. When money was scarce for the family, Mrs. Holness, Teacher's wife, told them of the possibility of the daughter, Mary, becoming housekeeper for the Irish policeman. Unfortunately, Mary also became Ella's mother. As a child, Ella had a difficult time growing up in Grove Town. As a mulatto child, she was snubbed by most of her classmates. They called her "Salt Pork," "Alabaster Baby," and "Red Ants Abundance." And when the new dance ring game "O'Grady Says" started, they called her "Ginger." She never played with her classmates and was not thought well of by most teachers, so she lived mainly in her imagination.

Ironically, Langley and his family fall into the line of Anansesem more than Ella, the heir to the Ashanti tradition of the trickster spider Anancy.[18] She was the fooled one who soon realized that there would be no real sex; Langley saw her merely as a prophylactic and did not accept her reality as a person. He used her, but they would have no child together; he still accepted the myth of the superiority of his race and was not ready to become the father of a person of color. The idea that they would not have children further distanced the two and brought Ella to the understanding that her dreams would never be fulfilled.

Ella finds that after sharing information with her husband about the characters and her experiences of her home in Grove Town, Selwyn is going to put on "the biggest coon show ever."[19] After going to the opening performance of *Caribbean Nights and Days* with Selwyn, Ella says to herself, "It didn't go so."[20] Her loss is so great that Reverend Brassington, the Methodist Grove Town minister, whose wife had talked him into taking Ella into their house for her growing-up years, travels all the way to New York City to bring her back to Grove Town and, in spite of his Methodist training, he takes her to be healed by the Myalist, Mass Cyrus. Reverend Brassington's decision to take Ella to the Myalist for healing is evidence that even he, a staunch Methodist, had begun to accept the power of the folk religion and culture.

The second story of spirit theft in *Myal* is the elder spirits' saving of the young woman Anita, a story of obeah and its undoing by devotees of the Kumina or Myal religions. Teacher Holness first mentions Anita's name in the second chapter when he listens to his student Ella O'Grady recite the British poem "The Steamers," based on Kipling's "The White Man's Burden." Teacher says, with "a mixture of gladness and stale amazement, "Not even Anita could do that."[21] Anita is his favorite student, so brilliant that he is busily planning to keep her in his school as a pupil-teacher,[22] now that she has reached the limit of the Jamaican public education, which ends when the student is fifteen years old. Since she is fifteen, Teacher has made her a "monitor" at his school, and he hopes that the inspector will budget the money to pay her to become a pupil-teacher.[23] She is going to his evening classes to prepare for the pupil-teacher exams, as Karl did in Pollard's *Karl*, and he is also teaching her "the rudiments of music."[24]

She is practicing her music and learning her notes when she hears the ping of stones being thrown against the zinc roof of the house rented by her mother. The pings make discordant notes against the harmony of her music, and finally, she opens the door to see what is going on, saying, "Is who throwing stone on the house at this time of the evening? . . . You boys stop it."[25] In her mind and that of her mother, boys who like her and admire her body are apparently throwing stones to get her attention. It is rather surprising, though, when one of the stones hits her in the middle of her forehead and then on her collarbone as she stands in the doorway. She tells her mother when she comes home from work, and her mother, Euphemia, tells her she must share this with Teacher. The mother grows more worried when the daughter is also bothered at night, even screaming out from her bedroom, in the early evening and again in the middle of the night. It was as if some man was in bed with her and demanding her body, although Anita never says so.[26]

Mass Levi is Euphemia's landlord and seems concerned that someone is damaging his roof with the stones, but he is throwing them himself, as becomes clear later. A prosperous farmer in Grove Town, he is also the money man in the community. He was District Constable before retirement and was always strict with everyone. He uses his horse-drawn cart to take women and their goods to market in the morning and to bring them back in the evening. He uses his cow whip to make sure his horse goes at a rapid pace across the bridge that he must cross to go from Grove Town's marketplace. The narrator lets the reader know that, as notable and powerful a citizen as Mass Levi is, he also has an eye for women, and while correcting them regularly, he is also teasing them. "Control, Miss Madeline, control," he says disapprovingly, and would not mind winning the tease.[27]

Brodber brings together all the forces of the elder spirits and living ministers of the Baptist and Methodist churches as well as the Kumina priestess, Miss Agatha Paisley, and the Myalists to help the innocent Anita remain in control of her body and mind and fight against the Obeah-driven currents against her. She introduces the subject of spirit thieves as Reverend Simpson, the Baptist minister in Grove Town, busily works to write his Sunday sermon. His text is "Let my people go." Also, Reverend Simpson briefly reflects on Marcus Garvey, whom he has just heard about, as "that fellow in St. Ann. Fellow that start up this Aboukir Institute."[28] He then thinks back to the far distant past in Africa when Europeans came and stole the Africans' stools.[29] He gets a message from Mass Cyrus, the Myalist healer, that the Baptists need to hold a deacons' meeting to get their forces together because he hears that Ole African is present. Reverend Simpson moves fast on his horse, Betty, to meet with his friendly spirit, Perce (Mass Cyrus), to talk about the present troubles and remember their triumphs of resistance in the past.

Reverend Simpson remembers a time five hundred years earlier when the slave ships ("those tacky old ships") had come to Jamaica.[30] He remembers that the higher spirits were present also on that Easter Sunday in 1760 when the historical Tacky's Rebellion took place. According to Bill Evans, Tacky was "a Coromantee chief from the Guinea area of the West Coast of Africa" before being enslaved in Jamaica.[31] Along with his followers, Tacky took over the Frontier and Trinity plantations in St. Mary Parish, killing their masters and others before stealing ammunition and firearms. Finally, they were caught and beheaded, and, as Evans writes, Tacky's head was "displayed on a pole in Spanish Town." The higher spirits have met throughout the succeeding generations. Reverend Simpson says they should take the high road and let Maydene Brassington take the low road, and they will beat her to Grove Town. They remember talking to Willie (Ole African) and know that he will be there to help.

Simultaneously, Anita's mother, Euphemie, is trying to calm her daughter by sleeping in her bed with her. However, her mind is far off as she thinks about Anita's father, who had not married her because his mother thought she was not good enough. The next man she loved, Taylor, was now planning to marry Mary (Ella's mother), whom he had loved all the time. While Euphemie is lost in these daydreams, a nightmarish vision appears: "A scarecrow was hanging from top to bottom in the doorway, its arms stretched out so that it seemed as if it were a rugged cross." The stones hit him, making him bleed, and soon he is gone, leaving his blood-wrenched shut-pan on the steps to verify that a human, although also spirit (an ancestral spirit), had been there.[32]

The symbolism of the scene suggests that this appearance is the spirit of Ole African, and he is overseeing the situation of Anita and the spirit thief who is attempting to take her spirit and her powers. He will right things as Jesus Christ did on the cross on Good Friday. At other times in the novel, the narrators refer to Good Friday and Gethsemane as well as other Biblical scenes and persons, such as Saul and Paul and the Witch of Endor.[33] Brodber indicates that the Judeo-Christian religion and African-inspired syncretic religions often work together and that there are various ways of knowing.[34]

Even though Reverend Brassington is a traditional Methodist minister, he does not trust the scientific doctors completely. They believed that Ella had "black boil" or worms or something they could not cure, and he went to the "old hermit," Myalist Mass Cyrus, who could heal such psychic and physical diseases, as Ella had. Brodber often uses Biblical allegory in her fiction. Saul, in 1 Samuel 25:28–30, went to the Medium or Witch of Endor to help him speak to Samuel, who had recently died, even though Samuel had commanded that his people not consult the witches for assistance. The Witch of Endor brought back the deceased Samuel for his advice on how to win a war against the Philistines to save Israel. Similarly, Reverend Brassington, a Methodist minister, accepts the assistance of the major practitioner of Myal (Mass Cyrus) to save his adopted daughter, Ella, when he realizes that he cannot do it himself.[35]

Myal is practiced by the ancestral spirits—Willie, Dan, Perce, and Mother Hen—who have lived across generations from slavery and still communicate with each other even across long distances. Willie, who also presents himself as Ole African and as a pig, plays drums. His favorite expression is "The half has never been told." Dan is a dog and sings and plays the cymbals.[36] At the time of the novel, Dan the dog takes the form of the Baptist minister, Reverend Simpson. Perce, who is a chick and blows the trumpet, takes the form of Mass Cyrus, the Myalman who cures Ella. In their current bodies, the spirits act to help the living and bring their memories across distances. In the novel, Miss Gatha, the leader of Kumina in St. Thomas Parish, is also called Mother Hen, and she brings her dance to the music of the Myal team. During the novel, the group of spirits also accept Maydene Brassington, the white British wife of the biracial Methodist minister, William Brassington, as a member of their Myal caucus. They call her White Hen because, through her knowledge of the spirits and their ways from her childhood and the teachings of her father, a British Methodist minister, she can commune with the spirits.

It is revealed that Mass Levi—Euphemie and Anita's landlord—is secretly attempting to use Obeah to divest Anita of her youth and sexual powers. He is the one who is throwing the stones at her house and then somehow bodily moves into her bed when she moves over to live with Teacher Holness and his wife, Amy. Amy Holness starts to sleep in the bed with Anita to protect her, but she also feels another body in the bed.[37] It takes the complete team of Myal spirits and the worshippers of Myal and Kumina to break the strong Obeah power of Mass Levi. Mass Levi's wife, Iris, has grown suspicious of her husband, who stays long hours in his privy every day, and investigates the privy one day to see that he is holding a wooden doll made to look just like Anita, with a nail in her neck. Using his strong power, Mass Levi can enter the body of Anita at will while in his privy each day.[38]

The elder spirits meet again and plot how they must save themselves and Anita from the spirit thief Mass Levi. Ole African (Willie) comes in from his house on the outskirts of Grove Town; Dan (Reverend Simpson) tells Willie that he received his message. Dan and Willie repeat the novel's refrain, "The half has never been told" and "They stole our sound."[39] But then they plan their strategy "to beat back those spirit thieves."[40] At 7:30 p.m., Willie reminds the spirits of the following verse from Thessalonians 3:2: "That we may be delivered from unreasonable and wicked men; for not all men have faiths." Melvin Rahming writes that "Spirit is Myal's epicenter."[41] The community of ancestral spirits meets several times during the novel because of the need to save both Ella and Anita from spiritual theft.

The ancestral, or elder, spirits have gotten in touch with each other at many disastrous times in the history of the African diaspora, such as in the kidnapping of Africans who were taken to the New World and during times of slave rebellion. These ancestral spirits use African-derived beliefs such as Obeah, Voodoo, Kumina, and Myal, which remain valuable energy sources to enforce beliefs and strengthen community resistance against spiritual theft.

The spirits are hosted by various bodies at different times. Willie, one of the oldest spirits, continues to reappear and to remind the other spirits and human beings that the spiritual life of beings still exists and can save persons in the present. "The half has never been told," Ole African reminds all of those people in danger of losing their spirits and lapsing into a state of becoming zombies. Ella and Anita are saved because of the force of the higher spirits. After her restoration, Ella will become a teacher and assist other younger Jamaicans to survive the still-living tricks of colonial education, which threaten to persuade the young people that their lives are restricted by the rules of thought, spirit, and behavior demanded by the colonial powers.

The next morning Miss Gatha (Agatha Paisley, priestess of Kumina) does her special dance in her long green dress with tiny red flowers and her head tie of the same print, big wooden circles in her ears, and a bunch of oleander in her hands. She dances to her tabernacle, taking long steps. Music and dance are important to the religious traditions of Kumina and Myal.[42] As they hear Miss Gatha's song, people from all over Grove Town and as far as Morant Bay join in with their instruments and especially drums. Their music stifles Mass Levi on his privy: "He was boxing and kicking off these sounds and those feet out there thumping his chest."[43] He drops the doll and all his books. The performance outside grows larger and louder and continues into the night. At that point, there is speaking in tongues and a change of face in both Anita and Miss Gatha: "Anita had conquered Mass Levi, but Teacher was just able to catch her fainting form."[44]

The strength of the Myal followers and spirits of the past and present defeat the Obeah techniques of Mass Levi, and Mass Levi's intended zombification of Anita is foiled. At the end of Anita's story, old Mass Levi dies, and Anita is saved. Miss Gatha and Reverend Simpson announce, "It is finished."[45] In the other story of spirit theft, Maydene Brassington takes Ella to her birth mother, Mary, for a short time before bringing her back to her home with her husband, Reverend Brassington, and immediately walking back to Grove Town to speak to Miss Gatha in the tabernacle. Miss Gatha is lying on the floor after her day of worshipping and transformations. She has lost consciousness and, for a while, assumes the face and spirit of Anita before returning to herself. In other words, she is at least for a short while spirit-possessed by Anita.

Grove Town would have been surprised to hear Miss Gatha tell Mrs. Brassington: "Go tell them. It is finished. The spirit thief is gone."[46] That is, Mass Levi is dead. Miss Gatha then calls Mrs. Brassington White Hen and shows that she accepts Maydene as one of the higher spirits. Maydene is ecstatic. And finally, she tells the Holnesses and all the spirits that Mass Levi has died, due to the work of the higher spirits, but they cover it up, saying he suffered a heart attack. Then Reverend Simpson (along with the higher spirit Dan) says that he also will accept the spirithood of Maydene Brassington as White Hen.[47]

The novel, as June Roberts notes, includes "six years of Ella's life: interwoven with a few months of traumatic events in Anita's life."[48] She also notes that Anita is healed around 1913 and Ella in 1919. According to Roberts, Brodber makes the minstrel show that Selwyn Langley created to coincide with traditions of the Harlem Renaissance and makes his audience think about Zora Neale Hurston and her inventive writings of that period.[49] After being saved, Anita continues to work with Teacher Holness, and he is lucky enough to get a scholarship from the British government for her to go to a teacher training college for further training. Ella is cured by Mass Cyrus (Perce) physically and spiritually, with the use of herbs. Reverend Brassington's congregation questions how it was done. Now they think that Reverend Brassington is "backra" (mulatto) because he knew to ask Mass Cyrus, who was Myalist, not Methodist or professionally trained, to cure his adopted daughter. Then the Brassingtons find Ella a job teaching a class to children and helping the upper division of the school with sewing.

Ella teaches the children under the almond tree in the Grove Town schoolyard using the traditional Jamaican primer about "Perce the chick, Master Willie, Mr. Dan, and their peers on Mr. Joe's farm."[50] But Ella has changed: she resists teaching the stereotypical British dogma, which makes the children resist the old days of zombification with the colonizer or slaveholder (Mr. Joe) and the colonized ones (the enslaved people or animals on the farm). The members of the spirit team are exuberant to know that Ella will have a seminar in Whitehall (a government building) about the need for a change in the Jamaican primer and school education generally. Her papers will be filed there, and there will be change. Perce flies over, playing his trumpet, and Mother Hen says, "Different rhymes for different times / Different styles for different climes / Someday them rogues in Whitehall / Be forced to change their tune."[51]

LOUISIANA AND SPIRIT POSSESSION

Brodber's third novel, *Louisiana*, is both historical and mystical.[52] The name of the novel is particularly metaphorical, for it takes place in two Louisianas—the Louisiana region of St. Mary, Jamaica, the West Indies, and St. Mary's Parish, Louisiana, in the United States. Brodber's home village, Woodside, was adjacent to the Louisiana Estate, which was named Louisiana in honor of the property owner's wife, Louisa.[53] However, the novel's protagonist, Ella Townsend, soon learns during interviews with Mammy and others that she herself was born in Louisiana, Jamaica.

The novel begins with the voices from heaven that are repeated throughout the novel. The voices are of the dead: Mammy, or Sue Anna Grant-King from southwest Louisiana; Lowly Girl, or Louise Grant, Mammy's friend from Jamaica; and Ella Townsend, a Jamaican-born anthropologist from Columbia University in New York, who becomes a voodooist and the life force of the dead Mammy and Lowly

Girl. Like Zora Neale Hurston, as Brodber explained, Ella Townsend becomes a devotee of the religions of Voodoo and Myal after she arrives in the US state of Louisiana.[54] She believes that a sociologist or anthropologist must live the life that she studies to understand it in depth. Zora Neale Hurston, an anthropologist like Erna Brodber and Ella Townsend, studied Voodoo in Florida and the Caribbean and wrote *Mules and Men* (1935) and *Tell My Horse* (1938) about her studies. Hurston joined several voodoo groups herself before writing the books.

In *Louisiana*, Ella Townsend becomes the life force of Mammy and Lowly Girl when Mammy, the main informant of her study of African Americans of southwest Louisiana, dies. Gradually, a group of women known as "the venerable sisters" (Ella Townsend, Mammy, and Lowly Girl) become figuratively if not literally related. They certainly all understand each other and speak using each other's voices. The women are all "spiritually possessed," and there are no major differences between the living and the dead. Ella Townsend and Lowly Girl were born in Jamaica, and Ella Townsend shares the souls of the other two women. She eventually becomes known as "Louisiana." Through oral voices, sayings, and songs, the reader learns that the African-derived religion of Voodoo, or Hoodoo, and the mystical connections of the living and the dead were very much alive in both the Louisiana of the United States and of Jamaica.

The reader learns at the end of the novel that Mammy has been a political activist as well as a religious and social leader in her home parish of St. Mary's, Louisiana, as a leader of the New Orleans longshoremen's strike and a leader of the Marcus Garvey movements in Louisiana and Chicago. The student Ella is taken with the new technology of the tape recorder, which she is attempting to master. However, in addition to recording Mammy's voice on the tape, she also records the words of Louise from Jamaica, Mammy's young friend (who is deceased), the voice of Silas (Mammy's husband, also deceased), and Reuben, who becomes Ella's husband.

When Ella attempts to interview Mammy, the older woman is playing a game of cards called coon-can, an antecedent of rummy, which is like the Spanish or Mexican game *con quian*. Mammy, we are told, "had mastered the skill [of playing the card game] in the longshoreman's strike and had honed it to a fine art on Chicago's Southside."[55] The game is mentioned in the first chapter, when Ella says to Mammy, "I'm putting this tube round your neck, remember we talked about that . . . so I can get into my black box here all that you have in that head you're so determined to dry out in the sun. . . . Victrola, Lowly, and Coon Can it was."[56] But when Ella tries seriously to interview Mammy (both alive and dead), Mammy always takes the lead and attempts to find out more about the interviewer. Her attempts to find out if Ella is Jamaican, not a New Yorker as she insists, makes Mammy think of playing the card game and moving toward a win. She is on the right track, and soon Ella must admit that her parents were really from Jamaica and she had been born there, but she never learned much about the island from her parents, who carried her to New York when she was only fifteen months old.

When one of Ella's first interviews of Mammy ends, Mammy is confident that she has won the first segment of the coon-can game. She has found out essentials of the young Ella's history, and she has chosen her to be the lifeline for her and her "venerable sister," Lowly Girl: "The baby is turning. . . . One headwater is breaking."[57] Ella does not know it, but she is becoming the lifeline for Mammy and Lowly Girl, who are dead but alive in memory. She hears their voices and writes them down, so that future generations can read and learn what they have done. Ella also learns about herself because Ella, Mammy, and Lowly Girl are all related, either by their rural Jamaican ancestry or by their commonality because they are all members of the African diaspora. Instead of being interviewed by Ella, Mammy is busy interviewing the young researcher, Ella, and sizing her up to become "the horse" or "the rider," who will be the body and "medium" for the souls of Mammy and Lowly Girl when Mammy dies.

In fact, shortly after Ella begins her interviews with Mammy, the old woman surprisingly dies. After she dies, Ella thinks she must stop her investigation, but she soon realizes that the old woman speaks through her, for as she sits in church, she suddenly shouts out Mammy's repeated phrase, "Ah who sey Sammy dead," has a fit, and must be taken out of the church. While undergoing this experience, Ella feels that she is "in a kind of grotto" and sees a wide rainbow that a young Mammy with thick black braids ascends. The grotto is a picturesque symbol of the other world that Ella often enters and receives messages from after Mammy has died. She sees Mammy climbing on a rainbow in the numinous otherworld, her head full of the hair that she had as a young woman. The images and references to Jamaican folklore become much more vital in Ella's mind, as she receives the souls of the two women, Mammy and Lowly Girl, and becomes the living body or "horse" to bear their spirits. The transfer of souls, or soul possession, is an important belief of African spiritist religions, including Voodoo/Hoodoo, Obeah, Kumina, and Myal.

Ella asks herself if the medium being used is "thought transplant," "hegemony of the spirit," "celestial ethnography," or "the anthropology of the dead."[58] The narrator discusses all these possibilities in the novel. Ella says, "My mind had been spoken aloud while the recording machine was on." She is "a vessel, a horse, somebody's talking drum"[59] and now bears the spirit of Mammy and Lowly Girl. In Voodoo, or Vodun, the spirits of individuals have the power to cross boundaries of nationality, life, and death to know each other and communicate. Ella takes on their voices as well as their thoughts, and her body weakens in the transaction. Mammy (Sue Anna Grant-King) and Lowly Girl (Louise Grant) are ancestors of Ella Townsend Kohl (now married to Reuben Kohl, also an anthropologist), who later becomes known as Louisiana. As the New Orleans poet Brenda Marie Osbey writes, "May they never leave us / May the newly sanctified find their way home to us also. / May they feel well and be pleased with these offerings."[60]

Ella becomes possessed by the spirits of Mammy and Lowly Girl to such an extent that she begins to talk like them and express their favorite thoughts and songs. She is undergoing a case of New Orleans Voodoo. More important to Ella's initial role as anthropologist and researcher, she begins to hear the elder spirits as they tell stories of their pasts and the pasts of their ancestors. These historical and sometimes melodic expressions enter Ella's mind, but sometimes the expression comes through the tape recorder. Ella and her husband, Reuben, transcribe these verbal thoughts, memories, and musical expressions into written form, which eventually will be a book manuscript to be published as the book *Louisiana*.

Folk songs and sayings are repeated throughout the narrative and form the metaphors on which the novel is based. "Den ah who say

Sammy dead" is the novel's signature saying and a musical refrain. Ella says the lines loudly in the church during Mammy's funeral, and she does not know why. It is a phrase that she hears from Mammy but does not recognize as a part of her own experience until later when she listens to the sayings and songs of the seamen and others who come to the home of Madame Marie in New Orleans.[61] There, Mrs. Forbes, who attended to Mammy before her death, tells Ella she must seek to learn more about what her role in spirit possession is all about.

Much later in the novel, the reader discovers that the first time Ella heard the words to the community funeral song "Sammy dead, Sammy dead, Sammy dead oh" occurred when she was just a baby, and her grandmother, with whom she lived in Jamaica, had died. The folk song "Sammy Dead, Oh" is a funeral song and also a mento song that is popular enough for it to be called "A Jamaica Song."[62] The lyrics describe Sammy, a very successful farmer who planted corn so tall that it caused his neighbors to finally kill him because of their jealousy. However, people cannot forget Sammy, and they mourn his death and pray for his burial and redemption so that he will have peace.

In her novel, Brodber puts together successive waves of African, Caribbean, American, and South American migrations, stressing the importance of Marcus Garvey's ideology as a unifier of the African diaspora since the early twentieth century. In Jamaica Creole language, "Den ah who say Sammy dead" is also a paradigm for immortalizing Garveyism.[63] It is a constant call-and-response refrain that goes back to Ella's own experience and her cultural memory of a folk song. When Ella "gets over" or recognizes that she has "powers" to read people and to know the past and future, she repeatedly remembers this phrase from childhood.

After the death of Mammy, Ella becomes a reader and is more possessed by the spirits of Mammy and her friend Louise, Lowly Girl. She is successful in healing and helping others find purpose in life. Ella is only learning to know her power, which was apparently passed on to her by her spiritual ancestor, Mammy. Mammy reminds Ella of her own grandmother, and both older women are responsible for passing on their wisdom and their power. The mind of the community—with several minds working together, sometimes at odds, and sharing the folklore, songs, and sayings of its communal culture—becomes the framework of the novel. While Brodber is a social scientist working with data and communicating with her principal informants, her characters are also spirits transcending the world of time. In this narrative structure, the beginning of the novel is the end chronologically. The crossings of the characters and their ancestors from Africa to Jamaica and to Louisiana in the US have created the diasporic consciousness shared by the characters of the novel.[64]

The idea of diasporic consciousness proves itself in the meeting of minds and spirits that convene in the house of the Voodoo priestess Madame Marie. Her boarding house is where Mrs. Forbes, who was instructed by Mammy, sends Ella to get further instruction in African spiritual religions, so that she will grow in spirit and knowledge and become worthy of becoming the lifeline of Mammy and Lowly Girl after their deaths. Crews of seamen who came to Madame Marie's house were possibly associated with the United Fruit Company, which was important to trading bananas and other fruits from Jamaica and other parts of the Caribbean in the early part of the twentieth century.[65] When the seamen came, they invariably sang their songs, as did Madame Marie and soon Ella: "There were times when there was a great dispute. But Madame would say, 'That's our song' or 'Fellows where'd you hear that? That's ours,' and the battle royal went back and forth with Madame telling how far in her distant past she had heard it and it couldn't possibly be West Indian."[66]

When Ella hears one of the groups at Madame Marie's boardinghouse starting a chorus of the song "Ah, Who Seys Sammy Dead," she imagines that she is at her grandmother's house:

> My shoulders rocked like a little paper boat trying to balance itself in the sea. . . . I was seeing things as if on a rolling screen, a movie screen. I saw the yam vines, light green on the pale-yellow bamboo sticks; I saw the big brick oven; I saw the tombs, the barbecue; I saw the sand-dashed house, the tangerine tree close by it, rabbits opening their noses and sniffing and gobbling grass inside their meshed house.[67]

Referring again to the movie screen metaphor of *Jane and Louisa*, Ella undergoes a flash of memory in which she re-experiences the time when she was a nine-months-old baby in Jamaica and watched her grandmother fall on the floor immediately after putting her in the crib.

Another song that has an overwhelming effect on one of the residents of Madame Marie's boardinghouse is "Just Before the Battle, Mother," a song that had come to be associated with the death of soldiers on the battlefield during World War II. The piece becomes the source of great pain to Ben, one of the seamen who journeyed to New Orleans often, so much that he felt compelled on a later visit to share his grief with Ella, hoping to find relief. On a later trip, the song made him think of a young woman, one of his brightest students, whom he refused to marry when she became pregnant. When she said to Ben, "'Teacher what ah going do, please Teacher'—and with those words the moan of the frightened bird of a child,"[68] he had responded verbally and mentally:

> Lilieth, I don't know what to say, what is to be done? How far are you on? It doesn't matter. What shall I do? rhetorical questions under the sobbing under the notes of the organ for a life that had spelt foreign travel, further study and maybe somewhere down the line a settled family with this said Lilieth or someone like Lilieth, for you liked her, really did, sobbing over the notes of the organ.[69]

Lilieth's family then took her to Port Maria, where the girl had a failed abortion and died. Ben attended her funeral but had never forgiven himself. His telling Ella about this matter would perhaps bring him some peace.

While at Madame Marie's house, Ella remembers her childhood and the pain of "a dissociated child"[70] who was never able to accept the mother who had left her with her grandmother and then picked her up nine months after the grandmother died and took her to New York to grow up. She felt distant from both of her parents, who never seemed to accept her. After living in southwest Louisiana and then in New Orleans as a prophet and spiritualist reader, she wants to confront her mother but never does, even when she is finally summoned back to New York. There she sees only a lawyer who has been paid to handle commercial matters after the parents have returned to Jamaica to live in a nursing home, far from the daughter who has been a great disappointment to them.

The parents are disappointed because Ella never wanted to become the medical doctor that they had wanted her to be. In addition, she did not finish her PhD in anthropology at Columbia University, but traveled to southwest Louisiana to work on a social science research project and never returned to live in New York. Ella had not even returned the expensive recording machine that the fellowship had credited her with because the more technologically advanced people that she met at Columbia when she and Reuben finally attempted to return the recorder did not know what it was. Her parents had paid for the recorder in the earlier years to protect her name and their own. The attorney shares all this information with Ella when she finally goes to New York to visit her parents but misses them because they had moved back to Jamaica. When Ella dies and her husband flies to Jamaica to tell her parents, they call him a *samfie* man (a trickster) who ruined their daughter with his sleight of hand.[71]

Brodber includes historical and political events that framed the lives of Jamaicans and African Americans, particularly those people who lived in St. Mary, Jamaica, and St. Mary's Parish, Louisiana, in the United States. They are related through their participation in the lives of African spirituality and resistance.[72] Brodber's characters in *Louisiana* are all involved in resistance battles, either in Jamaica or America, particularly through the Marcus Garvey movement or his Universal Negro Improvement Association (UNIA), along with mystical ideas of the past involving memories of Garvey and his ideas of diaspora and Pan-Africanism. Before the end of the novel, the narrator points out that all the major characters—Mammy (Sue Anna Grant-King), Lowly Girl (Louise), and Silas (political activist and husband of Mammy)—were all active followers of Garvey.

Ella attempts to research the official history of the Black people of southwestern Louisiana, but after Mammy dies, she learns much from the tape recorder and through the pendant that her husband gave her for their fifth wedding anniversary. Afterward, she has been brought in fully as the lifeline of Mammy and Lowly Girl, "the venerable sisters." Through the pendant, as Roberts explains "she finds an oral, embedded, suppressed social history of the Garvey movement, told from the inside by the dead former members."[73]

Slowly and by various means, mostly through oral discourse and social history of the dead, Ella learns about these people, how they are linked, and how they pass on their views. Lowly Girl was twenty years younger than Mammy. They met in the kitchen of a rooming house in Chicago, and Lowly tells her story to Ella in a very convoluted manner. She tells Mammy that they share the same last name of Grant. Even though Mammy's and Lowly Girl's voices appear in the first chapter of the novel, in the opening section called "I heard the voice from Heaven say," and their funerals are described as very similar, with mourners coming in from the UNIA and other groups from the community, accompanied by banners, Mammy and Lowly Girl do not tell their stories much until they speak through the pendant, which Ella wears when she has definitely "gotten over" and has taken on the name Louisiana (for the birth names of the two women, Louise and Anna).

Mammy reveals her story to Ella and the reader shortly before Lowly Girl reveals hers. After washing off the tapes of the tape recorder, as Anancy's wife had washed the magic pot that he had given her for cooking, things work differently for Ella than for Anancy's wife. The pot possessed no more magic for Anancy's wife after she washed it, and there were no more free dinners, but Ella hears more than ever from the dead women. Ella feels that she must accept the words of the tape recorder as Anancy's wife should have accepted the acts of the magic pot. She should not worry about doing the right thing and returning the recorder, which was not hers. Ella says to herself:

> I just prepared myself to transcribe once more and prepared myself for a new kind of devotion to this work. This instalment was shorter than the first. Within two weeks I had caught what I call the "current all" for it does appear that magic pot cannot be cleaned.[74]

First, Mammy tells the story of her grandfather Moses, who got into quite a squabble with his slaveholder, who had always enjoyed talking with him and telling him that slavery was not too bad. Moses had never thought about the word "slave." Hearing the word opened his eyes, and he told the slaveholder, "Massa sleep on the featherbed and we on the moss."[75] Then things got worse. Moses left the plantation and slavery. Massa sent the dogs to find him, and they brought him back. When Massa told him in a clear way, "You is a common slave. You is mine,"[76] the status quo did not work. Moses ran off again, was caught, and was killed by hanging. Massa Sutton, who had grown up with Moses, could not reconcile himself to this act and killed himself. Afterward, when Ella hears the song "Sammy dead" and remembers her own past (in her subconscious), she remembers how much Mammy had reminded her of her grandmother. Soon she is accepted fully into the role of voodoo priestess and hears more of Mammy's story.

When Ella, now also known as Louisiana, realizes that she is a Voodoo "reader," who will one day be expected to take over the role and clientele of Madame Marie, she begins to read the Bible more carefully, as Madame Marie does, even though Madame Marie is a voodooist. Ella is particularly interested in the story of Elijah and Elisha and the story of the Witch of Endor. She knows that when Madame Marie passes, she will play the role of Elisha, who was given the mantle of seer by the prophet Elijah:

> Right now there's a pay-off in doing it my way. For instance, me and the Elijah/Elisha story: here is definite recorded proof that what has been happening to me has happened to someone else before. . . . Let us build three tabernacles. Two dead people talking to a live one, just like Mammy and Lowly and me.[77]

Ella goes so far as to compare herself to the reappearing Elijah in the New Testament when Jesus Christ ascends to the mountaintop before three of his disciples, and God announces that Jesus is his son. Like Elijah, Ella is the voice of a prophet and can speak to the dead—in her case, Anna (Mammy) and Louise (Lowly Girl). Ella also compares herself now to the Witch, or Medium, of Endor, who appears in the First Book of Samuel of the Old Testament (1 Samuel 28:3–25). She was a living person with special powers who talked with the recently dead prophet Samuel because Saul demanded her to do so to get advice for him on whether he and his men should go to battle against the Philistines.

In following biographical data from Mammy after her death, Ella finds out about Mammy's life before her birth and the activities that much later took her from southwest Louisiana to Chicago and back to Louisiana again. We hear that Mammy's mother was the child of Moses, her grandmother's first husband, who had been lynched by his owner. Mammy and her mother would carry on his line of resistance. But first, Mammy's mother would fall in love with an Anancy character from Lafayette County in Louisiana, not far from her mother's home in St. Mary's Parish, Louisiana. This man, Ned Harris, sweet-talked the young woman, who was designed to become a teacher, before "Green turtle sitting by a hole in the wall," and who was seduced by Ned's tales about travel. Consequently, she went with him to New Orleans and became pregnant with Mammy-to-be. After the birth of her child, the young woman (Mammy's mother) went to work in the sugarcane field and became a leader in the resistance work of the cane farmers. She became a leader of the cane workers' strike on the Teche and was later hung.[78]

Mammy comes out of this generational line of resistance. Her work in the longshoremen's strike in St. Mary's Parish led her to leave the Louisiana area for Chicago, instead of being caught and possibly hung there as her mother was. In Chicago, she met Silas King, a Garvey leader. Mammy and Lowly Girl worked with Silas and later with the Garveyites in Louisiana before Mammy died there in St. Mary's as Ella interviewed her.

After taking on the name Louisiana and the spirit of the venerable sisters and transcribing their story and the stories of others that she met from Louisiana and Jamaica, Ella dies from a long illness. The lifeline of the diaspora weakens but is transmitted to future generations only as much as possible. The spirits of the ancestors teach resistance as well as survival in the continuing struggle of the diaspora.

Ella Townsend Kohl continues to listen to the tape recorder and to put her records together about Mammy, Lowly Girl, their husbands, and the people who told her their stories at Madame Marie's boardinghouse in New Orleans. However, Ella begins to grow increasingly weak and unbalanced, until her husband, Reuben, knows that "Louisiana, my wife, Ella Kohl . . . was going over the rainbow's mist with her knowing smile." After Ella's death, her husband returns to his home in the Congo of Africa. In the Prologue, the reader learns that Reuben has his lawyer from Chicago mail the manuscript of his wife's book, "Louisiana," to a publisher that was "looking for works on and of black women."[79] The book was published in 1974.

In *Myal*, Ella and Anita are subject to spirit theft, but they survive because of the elder spirits and the living culture and folklore. In *Louisiana*, Ella is subject to the spirit possession of Mammy and Lowly Girl and is made stronger because of her greater understanding of her culture and herself. In the Prologue, the reader learns that her book manuscript "Louisiana" has been published, and its readers know that there are more ways of knowing than are accessible to the five senses.

Chapter 4

MIGRATION, RETURN, AND "TOMORROW'S SPACES" IN VELMA POLLARD'S WRITINGS

Velma Pollard, an author of poetry, fiction, and nonfiction, writes about all the places that she has lived in or visited. Indeed, she explores the themes of migration, African Caribbean women, the new African Jamaican diaspora, and the next generation, which she calls "tomorrow's spaces."[1]

The term "diaspora" dates to Martin Delaney, Marcus Garvey. W. E. B. Du Bois, and others who believed that African culture lies behind the culture of places in the world where enslaved Africans were taken. In the twentieth and twenty-first centuries, the subject has come to be attached much more to the concepts of transnationalism, globalization, and hybridity. Sociologist Stuart Hall has written that "Afro-Caribbean people are already people of a diaspora" because of their diversity.[2] Brent Hayes Edwards discusses the historical and political history of the term and distinguishes it from the Pan-Africanism of Garvey and Du Bois and the Black Atlantic concept developed by Paul Gilroy.[3] Edwards points out that much of the writing of African American literature is diasporic and international in nature.

Pollard, like her sister, Erna Brodber, is interested in the cultural hybridity of the Caribbean, particularly Jamaica, but she also provides another view of what can be called "the new African Jamaican diaspora." My use of this term refers to the people of African ancestry who left the once-colonized Jamaica for education and job opportunities in the United Kingdom, the United States, or Canada. Dunn and Scafe's concept of "post-diaspora" described in the *Caribbean Review of Gender Studies*[4] is close to my concept of the new African Jamaican diaspora. Most characters in Pollard's fiction and poetry return to independent

Velma Pollard with calabash in her hand. Kunio Tsunekawa,
photographer, 2003. Courtesy of the Pollard Family.

Jamaica to find healing and a better chance of developing themselves
in their natural home.

In her novel *Homestretch* (1994), Pollard conveys the idea of the
nostalgia and "unbelonging" of the Jamaican couple David and Edith
in England and their return to their Jamaican rural homeland for a
new beginning in Woods Village, Jamaica, a fictional Woodside.[5] The
younger generation—Laura, David's niece; Laura's friend Brenda,
who grew up in the United States and England; and Anthony, who
had left Jamaica to attend universities of the United States—all return
to Jamaica at certain times to find their home and healing. Pollard's
poetry also has many settings, which include Jamaica, the US, the
UK, Canada, Belize, and the Virgin Islands.

HOMESTRETCH: MIGRATION, RETURN, AND THE NEW AFRICAN JAMAICAN DIASPORA

Homestretch has been added to the required reading list of students in Kenya's public schools because of Pollard's transnational appeal.[6] In the novel, Pollard deals explicitly with problems of migration and homecoming, as David and Edith return to Jamaica after thirty years of living and working in London. David, a carpenter, left Jamaica for a better job abroad but spent all those years working in a factory in London, where Edith, a teacher in Jamaica, worked as a practical nurse. Like the people who took the ship the *Windrush* from the Caribbean to Great Britain in 1948 after World War II,[7] they had high hopes for a good life abroad. Returning to Jamaica in their old age, the couple find new life with family and friends in their home in Woods Village. The description of the village and their roles in helping it find its earlier purpose and sense of community are based on Woodside and its community.

While the Woods Village of the novel is obviously inspired by Woodside and Pollard and her parents' experiences of the place, her two main characters, Edith and David, spend little time thinking about such feared things as "the terrible galliwasps" that live in the trees in Brodber's *Jane and Louisa*.[8] "If they bite you and get to water before you, then you are sure to die," says the narrator of Brodber's novel. Such unreal spirits and the practices of Obeah and other African-derived religions do live in the village, but Pollard does not emphasize them.

Edith and David have lived disappointing lives in England as practical nurse and factory worker, when they would probably have been a teacher and craftsman in Jamaica if they had stayed. Now at retirement, when David has just suffered a stroke, they return. But there are elements of the landscape of Jamaica that help David to recover, such as Milk River, where their friends Charley and Myrtle, who stayed on the island, take them when they return. The landscape is healing and restores David to several of his heretofore lost years. The couple regard the event of homecoming as a second chance to remember the ghosts of the past and to visit the graves of David's parents, but also to dig their feet deep into their church and the land of their ancestors.

Pollard begins her novel with an epigraph from the poem "The Heart's Metronome" by fellow Jamaican poet Dennis Scott: "It is time to plant / feet in our earth. The heart's metronome / insists on this arc of islands / as home."[9] The poem reflects the couple's return to their homeland after thirty years away. Most famous for his poetry collection *Uncle Time* (1973), Scott was daring in his poetic approach, but simultaneously loving of the past and his memories of home and environment. David Cowan, a scholar of West Indian poetry, writes: "Scott discerns a thread running through history as it runs through personal experience. . . . the yearning for freedom and self-realization ranged against the need to be connected to a community with a common focus worthy of love and admiration."[10]

Similarly, David and Edith had always planned this return, but their hopes for escape to their mother country turn out to be unrealized. While their home has changed and the Anglican church is far from the only church when they return, they observe signs of Pentecostal, Jehovah's Witnesses, Seventh-Day Adventist, Methodist, and Baptist churches. Seeing many of these church signs on their way to Milk River, they think about what they have heard about Jamaica and churches in the past: "'Jamaica has some kind of world record for churches per square mile, you know,' Edith says quietly, 'but I don't think we have any record for righteousness.'"[11] Even the Anglican service had been modernized. David and Edith view their homecoming as a chance to revitalize the Anglican home church and the community. They are welcomed as old members who would become excellent readers and leaders in the church.

David and Edith had been adventurous young people in the past. They had gone to England as "children of the empire,"[12] but that illusion was England's false call to its Commonwealth subjects. England was a horrible mother. It had wanted only laborers in its factories. When they return to Jamaica, Edith and David wonder if they should never have left. Perhaps they should have stayed, as their friends Charley and Myrtle had.[13] Many who went to England returned mad, such as the woman that they see standing in the door of a hut they pass while looking over their old home. It is Miss Betty's daughter, Avis, Myrtle and Charley tell Edith and David: "Nobody knows what happened over there [in England], but this is how she came back, and her brother who was sent for too is in a madhouse over there."[14]

The returned couple help to revive the church, the school, and the community. Edith meets with the young women of the church and teaches them how to keep up the altar. She helps them get rid of the "rat bats" in the church ceiling and the dingy atmosphere of the building. Edith also teaches the young parishioners the graces: how to make and give teas and how to live the better life, as she taught the young Jamaican women that she met in England. David picks up his mastery of carpentry and makes desks for the young students at the local school. He also enjoys growing plants and flowers in his garden that are native to the village.

David and Edith's home, Edaville, had once been Comfort Hall, the home of Edith's Gran, who is a major character in many stories and poems by Pollard and Brodber. David and Edith's home becomes a center of the new African Jamaican diaspora, which includes Laura, the niece of David's late sister; Laura's friend Brenda; and Anthony. Anthony becomes Brenda's friend and escorts her through many landmark areas of Jamaica. Laura, Brenda, and Anthony have spent important parts of their growing up years in other countries, but they return to Jamaica to find themselves and their families and to restore their own sense of self.

Laura suggests to her relatives that they plan a gathering with friends who want to welcome them back to their homeland of Jamaica. They should have held the gathering in October, the day before Heritage Week.[15] That way, they would see friends and would be able to renew their knowledge of the folklore and music of the nation. The novel is also a tour of Jamaica through its past and present and a story of its folklore and traditions, particularly its music. There is an overall description of place and the impact that it has had on the characters. The events would also give Brenda material that she could use in the article she was being paid to write on the culture and folklore of Jamaica. Brenda thinks that the events would also be a rich treasure for her teaching many young Jamaicans in her classes in England.

"You don't know the half," Brenda says to Laura. "I don't want those youngsters to continue to feel the way I felt. Placeless. Like you do not come from anywhere, certainly not England. It will be difficult. Just the amount of money we must find. But I know the others will buy the idea."[16]

The young people, accompanied by the older generation, David and Edith, go to the Mento Yard, where Brenda first hears Jamaican mento music, which helps to heal her terrible feeling of rejection by Jamaica.[17] She feels rejected because she was told to leave Jamaica by her mother and find a new life with her father, who, she felt, was always unreliable. In addition, her life in America and England was very disappointing. In Jamaica, she and Laura are happy to hear many of the musical and dance rhythms and to absorb the spirit of the area of St. Ann and St. Mary Parishes. Brenda decides that she will attempt to bring the young students she is teaching in England to Jamaica to view the historical landmarks of Woods Village. Brenda and Laura are absorbed by the Kumina religious group and several musical groups that they enjoy in the Mento Yard. The Kumina groups are playing music and dancing inspired by the Johnkunnu, Horsehead Maypole, and the Bruckins group, which incorporates the Manalva and its king and queen, the Emancipation Day festivities of August 1, quadrille groups, and other "Ninth Night" festivities. The festivities engage "the melodrama of putting motherland and diaspora rhythm and movement side by side."[18]

Homestretch has a linear narrative, with events moving from the beginning to the end with few flashbacks. On the other hand, Pollard's sister's novels are nonlinear: the plots are disjointed, and narrative time must be interpreted by the reader. In *Homestretch*, the individuals are carefully drawn as separate individuals with their own past and present, and, even though similar, the reader does not get the idea that the world of spirits is imminent, even when the author says so. The places in Jamaica that the characters visit are separate and carefully drawn to give the reader a tour of the country, the vegetation, the mythical characters, and the events with which they are associated. An example of the difference between Pollard's and her sister's use of the same cultural experience is the two writers' descriptions of the Manalva, a mythical figure in Jamaican folklore. Pollard depicts Laura showing the importance of the Manalva figure, who is the queen.

In the sword dance, the king and queen appear after the Bruckins musical group performs. Laura goes to find David and Edith, so they can see these performances as well. However, Pollard does not move away from the linear narrative. The Manalva and the sword dance remind Laura of the grief she still feels for her mother. However, Pollard does not take the reader away from the narrative for very long. She moves on to describe other parts of the Mento Yard performances.

Erna Brodber describes the Manalva in her novel *Jane and Louisa Will Soon Come Home*, when she discusses the attraction between Nellie, the novel's protagonist, and a friend of the family, Mass Stanley. He loves the chance to talk with the young girl, who was just going into puberty, about his past love for her Aunt Becca, whom he calls "Coolie Gal." Mass Stanley says to Nellie: "Chile, woman was sweet."[19] He begins the story by connecting Aunt Becca with Manalva, and he explains how "he used to ride a horse with his sword and shield to protect the queen [Manalva]."[20] Unfortunately, his brother Tanny also had an affair with Aunt Becca, which resulted in her becoming pregnant. Her pregnancy led to her having an abortion, a muted background story that recurs throughout the novel. Aunt Becca ended up marrying neither of the Ruddick brothers, Stanley or Tanny. She married a more prestigious and lighter-skinned man, Teacher Paddock. Brodber uses her description of Manalva and the sword dance to symbolize the lost love Mass Stanley once had for Becca and his nuanced attraction for the young Nellie because she reminds him so much of her Aunt Becca.

In *Homestretch*, Pollard describes her characters in a much more realistic fashion. Brenda is an important character in the novel. Pollard discusses her life of dislocation in almost as much detail as she discusses that of David and Edith. Darlene Schulenberg, in her MA thesis on Pollard's writings, describes this young woman's "dislocation" very realistically.[21]

Brenda spent the first fourteen years of her life with her mother, Joy, and her grandmother. But abruptly, she was separated from her mother and her native home and sent to live with her father, Ivan, in New York because he asked Brenda's mother to send her. He said that she would get a better education in the United States. Her mother did not want to send her away, but knowing the importance of education and money, she did. However, Brenda had a terrible time with her father's African American wife and their child, who both feel that Brenda must be a "helper who would assist them with domestic chores." She is not accepted at the school either but is expected to be a tutor to the other foreign students in her grade level. Brenda only begins to find herself when a woman employee in her father's business becomes her friend and helps her do well in school.

Another disruption, though, keeps her from feeling a sense of location. Her father divorces his African American wife and moves to England to marry a nurse there. He takes Brenda with him, and Brenda must find herself again; but because she has studied well in Jamaica and America, she begins to find her way in England. However, her sense of loss ends up pushing her into contact with various antisocial groups. Luckily, she gets into a journalists' group that hires her and assigns her to write a cultural history of her home country, Jamaica. At the first time she appears in the novel, she is very much at odds with the customs office at the Kingston airport when she arrives in Jamaica. However, she meets her friend Laura and is invited to the home of Laura's aunt and uncle, Edith and David. She begins to find herself and not to feel so rejected by her home, especially when she accompanies her new friend, Anthony, who is also visiting his native home while studying in the United States.

Eventually, Brenda visits her grandmother and mother in another parish of Jamaica. She finds that her mother has finally resumed her education as an adult (through a government program for continuing education). Brenda realizes that she has not been rejected by Jamaica or by her mother. Jamaica is still her home, even though she has spent a long stretch in other places. The novel ends with Brenda bringing her British students to her homeland of Jamaica, as Laura suggests. The young people of the new African Jamaican diaspora view the whole island as a rock, somewhat impenetrable. In Jamaican Creole, one of the youngsters says, "A di rock dis."[22]

Homestretch is Pollard's study of her home, a place that was lost to many but rediscovered as well. Brenda writes to her friend Laura when she leaves again for England that "Jamaica little but it tallawah."[23] The history and culture of her home will live forever in Brenda's mind, even though her time in Jamaica has been brief. As Stefano Bellin notes, *Homestretch* is a story of dislocation and a return to a sense of belonging, as it is in Brodber's *Jane and Louisa*, and a return to a sense of belonging, as it is in Brodber's *Jane and Louisa* and *Myal*.[24]

POLLARD'S POETRY AND "TOMORROW'S SPACES"

In my interviews with Velma Pollard and Erna Brodber in July 2005, Pollard explained how her interest in language derives from her parents' love of literature, something that is true of much of the community of Woodside. According to Pollard:

> My mother used book words in the community and at school. She was a teacher. She would know how to use words like *awry*.... My father spoke Creole. He was into amateur dramatics. A doctor who came from America and his son in Kingston came up to the country, and, together with my father, they formed a drama club. They would read and dramatize plays, such as Shakespeare's *The Merchant of Venice*. My father would play the trial scene, and he would proclaim:

> **Duke:** Make room and let him stand before our face.
> Shylock, the world thinks—and I think so too—
> That thou but lead'st this fashion of thy malice
> To the last hour of act....

> **Shylock:** I have possessed your grace of what I purpose,
> And by our holy Sabbath have I sworn
> To have the due and forfeit of my bond.[25]

Pollard continued, "Jumping from one side to the other, my father would sometimes play Portia saying, 'The quality of mercy is not strained; / It droppeth as the gentle rain from heaven.' And my father loved to tell Anancy stories. I can hear him say, 'When I say Splash, you must say Tip.'"[26] In her scholarly research, Pollard, a linguist, has demonstrated a sustaining interest in language, particularly Rastafarian language or "Dread Talk." She views Dread Talk as "a lexical expansion of Jamaican Creole and the linguistic expression of the folk."[27] In her poetry, Pollard's use of language in its many dimensions is apparent. The poem "Fly" in *Crown Point and Other Poems* (1988) begins and ends with the children's rhyme: "Ef a ketch im / A mash im / Ef a ketc im / A mash im."[28]

The poem imitates the sound of the railway train along the track. What seems at first reading to be the re-creation of an Anancy tale for children opens many levels of meaning. The speaker identifies with the fly falling for the seductive invitation of the spider to walk into its web. The spider is spoken of in the second person; therefore, the fly, who is caught in the spider's (Anancy's) web, is associated with the reader: "And I / the fly / inspecting your web." The "microscopic eye" of the speaker, reflecting her nearsighted, limited vision, sees only peace and serenity in the web; she enters and sleeps.

But, waking up, the fly finds herself trapped by the web—no longer able to "butterfly fly." She is just one of the many flies lost in the web and when she cries out to the spider (Anancy) perched outside, her cry is scattered; the distance to him is very distant. Anancy, the trickster, full of illusions, is also the singer of the nursery rhyme; he laughs at humans, particularly women—flies—lost and subject to his control in their blindness. Like Brodber, Pollard incorporates this kind of tale and character in her poems and stories.

The theme of marriage as a cage is a recurring motif in Pollard's poetry and short stories. Her first collection of short stories, *Considering Woman*, includes three stories in the section called "Cages," and she adopts Derek Walcott's lines from his *Joker of Seville* as section epigraph: "You beasts must love your cages."[29] In her poem "The Fly" in her first book of poetry, *Crown Point and Other Poems*, the woman is a victim of the spider, who keeps her there in his web. But if the woman/fly had not been interested in the interaction, she would not have come into the spider's control. In the poem "Anansa" in *Crown Point*, the woman is Anancy herself. She weaves many threads to keep her husband in the house, but as Odysseus leaves Penelope to win his glory, not just once but twice, the man in the poem must depart. The woman fails to keep him home. In this poem, everyone is a "tiif" (thief); no one has complete control: "The king tiif, the governor tiif / tiif, you tiif, all a / we tiif / The king is forever a woman."[30]

In Pollard's poetry, she often expresses herself through what Edward Kamau Brathwaite has labeled "nation language" and what she calls Jamaica Creole.[31] Brathwaite (1930–2020), born in Barbados, was an academic, poet, philosopher, and poet. Very scholarly in language, he was also keenly interested in how Anglophone writers in the Caribbean had moved toward using nation language in their writings, instead of strict English. Brathwaite introduced the term "nation language" in relation to Caribbean language that had before often been called dialect or patois. But he felt that his term emphasized the language as part of an oral tradition that was based on sound and was closely related to the African traditions in the Caribbean.

In many of her poems, Pollard explores various parts of the Caribbean, such as Belize, Grenada, Cuba, and the British Virgin Islands, as well as the United States, particularly New York and Los Angeles. She describes the African diaspora and its spiritual existence around the world. The political world appears in many of her poems, as well as the natural world of hurricanes, water, and mountains. However, a recurring theme is family and the growth of the young people of the new diaspora of the Caribbean: these new generations would carry on the traditions of the culture. She calls these young persons "tomorrow's spaces," as I note in an essay in *The Xavier Review*.[32]

The poems about Gran and her husband, Corpie, Pollard and Brodber's maternal grandmother and grandfather, tell much about the life of the family in St. Mary, St. Catherine, St. Ann, and other parts of rural Jamaica. It was a life in which people believed in community and took care of the children and old folks. They believed in theater, music, and art. The sense of folklore and the life of the spirit can be seen in the rich literature, music, and political life of the region. In "Crown Point," the title poem of Pollard's first volume of poetry, the speaker shares memories of Gran and Corpie, who fought in the Boer War and returned to Benbow, near Guy's Hill, St. Catherine, full of memories of the war and the life abroad. In the poem, Gran speaks in her Anglican voice: "Bless the Lord oh my soul / and all that is within me / bless his holy name."[33] The speaker smells the *khus-khus* and sees the Bible, large and black with all the important family dates, open on the table. She continues, "And forget not all his benefits who forgiveth all thy iniquities / who healeth all thy diseases / who satisfieth thy mouth with good things."[34]

The speaker/granddaughter cannot hear all the words of Gran, however: "Perhaps the clutter of my / life / obscures her voice."[35] The clutter of the speaker's life is due to the many places and events in the diaspora that have claimed her attention, as she describes in this volume of poetry. She ends the poem: "Perhaps her mystic to me / waits my silence / waits my tomorrow's spaces." Pollard repeats the idea of "tomorrow's spaces" in several of her poems, including this volume's "Bud/Unbudded." That poem describes a flower as her buds open: "This flower sees me watch / her glory flaunted / This flower hears me pause and knows me pause / to grieve for her tomorrow's spaces," the petals that have fallen unbudded.[36]

The speaker refers to our inability to know what tomorrow will bring, but she knows that her journey has taken her far from Woodside to other terrains and cultures and to Africa, particularly Ghana. Several of Pollard's poems are about the death and spiritual life of the ancestors. The poem "After Adowa" creates a palimpsest of the Ghanaian funeral dance (the Adowa) and the Jamaican funeral song "Sammy Dead, Sammy Dead, O," which is used repeatedly by Brodber in her novel *Louisiana*. Both sisters point out the major influence that Ghana has on the culture and arts of New Orleans. The poem begins with "vaivan / vaivan," moans of the women as they do the funeral dance, first to the spirit within, and then to the drums, gourds, whistles, and fifes of the family and community.[37] The Adowa is a funeral dance that Ghanaians perform, as New Orleanians often perform their "second line" dance after a funeral as they move toward the burial. It is a way of accepting the future that is unknown but connects people to the other world and carries them in, one by one: "vaivan / vaivan / the woman hears 'Sammy dead . . . O.'"

Many of Pollard's poems develop an understanding of the closeness of the African diaspora in terms of religious and communal traditions. She is simultaneously concerned with the common political and social concerns of the peoples who inhabit the Caribbean, particularly the people who have known British colonialism—for example, people of Belize, Grenada, Guyana, the Virgin Islands, and Jamaica. In many of her poems, she discusses colonialism and the far distant past of the first European discoveries, as in the sequence that she calls the "Virgin Island Suite." The suite includes "I. Drake," "II. Drake's Strait

Revisited," and "Drake's Strait Remembered," all with reference to Sir Francis Drake, one of the earliest British explorers.[38] She thinks how strange it is that Drake's name is still used, after six hundred years, to mark an important strait in the British Virgin Islands, a major tourist attraction in the Caribbean.

In the first poem of the sequence, the speaker says that people of the Caribbean always remember "the pirate buccaneer" Sir Francis Drake, who captured the treasure of the Caribbean, South America, and Spain, traveling all the way from the Atlantic to the Pacific Ocean and taking the treasure back to Queen Elizabeth I and England. In the second poem, "Drake's Strait Revisited," the speaker says, "I am here for Drake, / To feel his passage once again."[39] The speaker wants to return to see and feel the awe that these lands and waters must have had for Drake and Columbus. Columbus named these islands Virgenes, not the name given to them by the Tainos or Arawaks, the indigenous people who first populated the islands. The British, the Danes, and the Americans would take over the property and give them new names—such as St. John and Tortola. In the third poem, "Drake's Strait Remembered," the speaker points out that these islands and waters have gone through many changes; sometimes, the islands are viewed metaphorically as "a green girl in the ring / tra la laa."[40] Women of Jamaica are often described as such in Brodber's novel *Louisiana*.

In another sequence of poems, Pollard writes about Caribbean places because they are historical landmarks of the diaspora. One of these sequences is the "Belize Suite," which consists of three poems: "Sea Wall," "Xunantunich," and "Road from Xunantunich." The Xunantunich is an ancient site in western Belize, home of several pyramids built by the Mayans. The location is here described as quiet and dark; at the water's edge, the beach enjoys the gentle winds of a peaceful time. But there have been loud and tumultuous times of hurricanes and earthquakes.[41] The area is silent with no trees and no mountains. Living there would be impossible except for tourist guides and people who service the tourists. However, tourists have given these landmarks new meaning, as they come to climb the pyramids and lay offerings there. Tourists who climb the pyramids realize, like the Mayans who built these pyramids for their gods, that to keep their power, they needed to look down on the people who planned to conquer them. In the second poem of the sequence, "Xunantunich," the tourists all go home but are sobered by the power and mystery that they have experienced: "Power is always from on high / lookouts where pirates guard the harbor / rivers that tumble down from angry hills / cloud tops for cherubim."[42]

Another sequence of poems leads to the title of her 2013 volume of poetry, *And Caret Bay Again*. Pollard has been "strongly affected by her visits to the British and the US Virgin Islands, Gorda and Caret Bay in St. Thomas, particularly. She admits feeling an obsession [for those places]," writes a reporter in *The Jamaican Gleaner*.[43] The first two of her Caret Bay poems are also found in Pollard's poetry collection, *Shame Trees Don't Grow Here* (1991). In the first poem, the speaker describes the beautiful and historic landscape of rocks, bamboo, and sand on the ocean of Belize. The poet describes the landscape in geometric designs: "Stone cabbages / Fulformed from rock face / Burst endless."[44] "Caret Bay (Again?)" is the third poem of that suite. In this poem, the speaker remembers the beauty of the place and the love that she felt as a young woman. Now she is an older woman but is still able to walk around the rocks and enjoy the memories. She continues to walk along this water's edge. The beauty and the peace of this place survive: "Morning rocks / . . . Cool sands / Pelicans and peace / At Caret Bay."[45]

Pollard also writes poems about the old colonial power, England, and the ways that colonial power has moved to incorporate itself in the cultures of its many Commonwealth nations. In "BM [British Museum] Revisited," the speaker points out that the sculptures of the Parthenon are mere "empire fragments" and there is equally significant art from the independent nations, earlier colonized by the British, such as Jamaica. This art shows the history of the peoples who compose their nation, such as the quilt of a woman whose grandfather was Ashanti, shards of a vase from China from a man whose grandfather was Han Chinese, and the dances that bear African rhythms and European names, such as the quadrille and the schottische. These "hodgepodge wholes" contain a better center— Jamaica—and their axis revolves around other places, which are a part of the histories of the people of the present generation.

In her poetry, Pollard also confronts the matter of power and resistance that people of the Caribbean faced in the latter half of the twentieth century as nations moved away from colonial powers toward independence. One of the leaders of this time was Walter Rodney, a revolutionary with a message of independence to the countries of Africa and the Caribbean in the 1960s and 1970s. Rodney, born in Georgetown, Guyana, in 1942, was a well-known scholar and activist during the 1960s and 1970s, renowned for his scholarship and speeches on behalf of the oppressed peoples of Africa and the Caribbean.[46] He taught at UWI for several years before publishing his first book, *Grounding with My Brothers*, and gave lectures and discussions on behalf of working people. After attending a conference in Montreal, Canada, in 1964, he was barred from returning to Jamaica, and riots followed on the island.

Rodney began teaching in Tanzania, on the continent of Africa, and continued his studies and speaking about African liberation and Pan-Africanism. In 1972, he published his most famous work, *How Europe Underdeveloped Africa*, which is considered a classic about colonialism.[47] Later he returned to Guyana, where he became a voice of the people in his political group called the Working People's Alliance, which was associated with a number of strikes and was labeled by the establishment as socialist practice.

He was assassinated by policemen on June 13, 1980, in Georgetown, Guyana, a subject of concern in Pollard's poem "After Rodney" in two parts: "Black Friday" and "From the Wife," in *Shame Trees Don't Grow Here*.[48] "Black Friday" is the name given to the day that Rodney was assassinated. In Pollard's poem, the speaker asks a series of rhetorical questions: "Do you not fear / who sent his ashes / on the wind / that ashes blow / more wild / than words?"[49]

Rodney's assassination made him a martyr whom people began to know about in Africa and all over the Caribbean; however, he had scattered seed that would grow—not just his three children, but his words and thoughts of liberation. In the second part of the poem, Rodney's wife says that she has no tears now because they will not bring him back to his life or serve as justice for his death: "So now I keep my tears / their salt to season / my resolve / preserve my centre."[50] The wife is strong, and the salt of her tears—"sucking salt" as literary scholar Meredith Gadsby calls it[51]—will preserve her strength and fulfill the realization that she and her children are the new center of the diaspora: the center that the British colonizers once held, but the new day had come.

Pollard's volume *Leaving Traces* includes several poems about time passing; the speaker is growing older, and the children and grandchildren will soon take over. In "Cut Language," the speaker talks to her grandson about understanding his "Jamaica creole language" and the language of his adopted country, the United States. She laughs when she realizes that he is a "wordsman" and already knows both styles of language, perhaps through his family and friends, and he speaks both every day. When some of his neighbors offend him, he says to them, "gwe bwai / no bada wi. / didn't I tell them / every time / bilingual is the lick?"[52]

The speaker's grandchild has learned to speak Jamaica Creole language to show his pride in the Jamaican nation language, even though he has grown up in Canada and the US, where his neighbors look down on Jamaica Creole or patois. In many of her poems and her fiction, Pollard uses various styles of English—Standard English, Jamaica Creole, and Dread Talk. She is an expert in all these ways of talking and understands the reasons that people use one or the other or several, proclaiming their identity with the use of each one. The poem "Cut Language" also echoes an important part of Pollard's message. In most of her poetry and fiction, she is interested in understanding her "tomorrow's spaces" and the new African Jamaican diaspora.

Similarly, Pollard's sister, Erna Brodber, is interested in the passage of time and the changes that one experiences as one comes out of the *kumbla*. Pollard knows migration like that of the characters of *Homestretch* but also realizes the healing effect of returning to one's home and family. *Homestretch* explains the emptiness and sterility that the older couple knew in England and the healing and love that they feel on coming home after thirty years. The young people Laura, Brenda, and Anthony also feel the need to go away and know the world, but they feel the warmth of what it means to return as well.

In her poetry and fiction, Pollard expresses her understanding of language, folk culture, and religion, but also the importance of travel and knowledge of various places and cultures.

ERNA BRODBER'S *THE RAINMAKER'S MISTAKE* AND *NOTHING'S MAT* AS AFROFUTURISTIC AND SPECULATIVE FICTION

In two of Erna Brodber's later novels, *The Rainmaker's Mistake* (2007) and *Nothing's Mat* (2014), she creatively speculates on the development of the diaspora and family history. Time- and space-shifting are important in both novels. In fact, both novels are speculative or Afrofuturistic fiction in form and thought.

Speculative fiction is defined by more than time- and space-shifting. As Annie Neugebauer writes, speculative fiction is a genre that is opposite to realistic or mimetic fiction, and it can include "fantasy, science fiction, and horror."[1] It is a fiction that asks, "What if?" In *The Rainmaker's Mistake*, what if human beings could be produced from yams? In *Nothing's Mat*, what if a human could be born that looked like a callaloo plant? What if people could move in time and space from the past to the present and future in their lives? What if a story could have seven narrators instead of one? These questions are asked in Brodber's later novels.

According to Ytasha Womack, in *Afrofuturism: The World of Black SciFi and Fantasy Culture*, "Afrofuturism is a term coined by cultural critic Mark Dery, who used it in his 1994 essay 'Black to the Future.'"[2] Womack also points out that the roots of the aesthetic began decades earlier with African American writer Martin Delany and later with science fiction writer Octavia Butler and musicians Sun Ra and George Clinton and that Afrofuturistic fiction is about African American people and their history and exists on many levels.[3]

The village of Woodside in St. Mary Parish, Jamaica (Brodber and Pollard's home) is the lens for the terrestrial and extraterrestrial spaces of *The Rainmaker's Mistake* and *Nothing's Mat*. In *The Rainmaker's Mistake*, Brodber fashions an original creation myth that has many parallels with the creation story of Genesis and yet is also a fable of slavery and emancipation, as well as a projection of what will happen to people of the African diaspora in the future. The young newly freed people find that the yam story is not literally true, but part of the myth that explains "the historical and metaphysical connection between humans and the soil."[4] Queenie, the main narrator, and her friends find themselves in the world of the free, and they learn more about their ancestral history, all the way back to Africans being taken into slavery.

In *Nothing's Mat*, the main narrator, Princess, the daughter of Jamaican parents, who was raised in Great Britain, discovers her ancestral and family history in Jamaica. She finds that she is a part of a long ancestral history and a large and growing diaspora, whose members have settled in various parts of Jamaica and much of the Caribbean, Panama, the United States, Canada, and the United Kingdom. Princess finds the history of much of her family by becoming a friend of her Jamaican cousin, Nothing, also known as Conut. Family relationships extend throughout the diaspora and include products as unbelievable as the child of Conut's friend, the callaloo plant. Princess learns much about the diaspora of her family from Conut's mat (her family tree) and passes it on to the new generation.

THE RAINMAKER'S MISTAKE: MYTHIC PORTRAYALS OF SLAVERY AND EMANCIPATION

At the beginning of *The Rainmaker's Mistake*, the narrator describes Mr Charlie, a white Jamaican slaveholder, looking out on his expanse of a thousand acres and remarking on the budding plants—the poincianas and the many little poincianas they had spawned. (In the novel, the "Mr" in Mr Charlie is written without a period.) He observes the corn, cassava, and plantains and is obviously happy with his creation. Like God in Genesis, he proceeds to describe the later creation of his human laborers. Inspired by the proliferation of plants growing so fully on his plantation, he is proud that he could generate humans as well. He makes himself believe in the yam story, which he tells his enslaved laborers. The narrator (Queenie, one of the young laborers) tells the story to the reader:

> Eyes glazed and looking into the future, he pulled his shirt out of his trousers, loosened the flap of his fly, knelt down and with fingers roughened and hardened by tedious labour, he dug a hole in the ground and planted a wash of seed from his body.[5]

Mr Charlie tells the story that he unites his seed with the earth to produce people who are associated with the earth. They were yams that grew underground first, as tubers, and then above ground. They grow up to be his enslaved laborers, and they will grow yams themselves, as they grow older. Yam was thought of as a sustenance food and was the preferred food of West Africans and their descendants. As Elizabeth DeLoughrey points out, yams were the first food planted and the last during the harvest season.[6] The crop was always planted in the provision grounds, along with callaloo, sweet potatoes, and other staple products, while white sugar, coffee, tobacco, and other foods most important to Europe and the capitalist nations were planted on the outskirts of the plantation or farm and took much labor. Yams, writes DeLoughrey, became a metaphor for transplantation of "root, as well as food culture because it was a crop from the African past and the new world as well." The yam festivals of the Igbo people of Ghana and Nigeria were also celebrated in Jamaica and other Caribbean countries.[7]

Readers learn in the final chapter of *The Rainmaker's Mistake* that Woodville, the overseer, had been the spirit Tayeb in Africa. He had ultimately caused the Africans to be captured and enslaved. However, through most of the novel, readers and the servants of Mr Charlie thought that Woodville was Mr Charlie's second-in-command and foreman. Readers do not find out until the final chapters that he was inhabited by the African ancestral spirit Tayeb. Africans who were stolen into slavery and transmitted to the West were accompanied by ancestral spirits, as is true in the novel *Myal*.

There are seven narrative voices in *The Rainmaker's Mistake*, although the prevalent voice is Queenie, who is one of the young, enslaved laborers. However, her learning throughout the novel is also reflected in the experiences and narrative voices of other characters. Early on, Queenie describes the situation of Mr Charlie: "Yes, there was more than this to life, he thought and said aloud: 'I need labour.'"[8] Through viewing the things of nature, particularly the "phallus-like dependents of each flower, an idea popped in his head."[9] Queenie recounts what Woodville told her fellow laborers about their birth from yams, but knowing that the reader might be quite skeptical about all of this, she adds, "We began as yams. Mr Charlie's seeds turned into yams, in us. OK?"[10] Queenie explains that the infants were raised by big sisters. Mr Charlie's plantation was a kind of Eden, and his laborers call him "Fount of Wisdom, Interpreter of Life, Father, Maker," loved by his creation, "who did Nothing without his orders" and depended on him for the meaning and pattern of their lives.[11]

But these religious appellations contradict the characterization that Mr Charlie is also a rich slaveholder.[12] In effect, all his "created" humans were his enslaved laborers, though Brodber never uses the word "slave" in the text. Every year, Mr Charlie enacted a familiar ritual of slavery on Founder's Day. He invited all his laborers to the Big House, and Woodville presented the new babies to Mr Charlie, who named them, with an eye toward Woodville to make sure that they were the right names. He then presented all these people with two gifts each—clothes and two dollars to the big sisters who took care of the babies. Queenie said that, on the Founder's Day of 1834, Mr Charlie came out on the verandah and made an announcement, particularly to the group who were to be in "the pickney gang" after the following harvest or yam season. This gang included all the laborers who were almost six years old, including Queenie, Little Congo, Phoebe, Essex, Jupiter, Juba, and the twins Castor and Pollox. Queenie says to the reader:

> Meet my special friends. We have experienced the same number of yam sessions and next season we will be in the pickney gang. Mr Charlie told us that this was the year 1834, that we were under six years old and now free. We smiled and waited. We always smiled when Mr Charlie talked to us, and he usually

smiled back. But Mr Charlie was not smiling. What to make of that? This is 1834. You are under six years old and you are free.[13]

Slavery was abolished twice in the Commonwealth nations of the United Kingdom. Enslaved persons were freed in 1834 to become apprentices to the slaveholders and still worked on the plantations. However, they were given their total emancipation in 1838. (See Chapter 1 in this book.) The yam people in *The Rainmaker's Mistake* were also freed twice. Queenie says that the *kaachi* horn was blown, and Mr Charlie announced to all the people of his plantation: "It is 1838. . . . You are free." Queenie adds, "Mr Charlie then left the verandah and walked through the door, not to be seen again."[14] This time Woodville was violently angry. First, he said, "Didn't I tell you you'd do that?" He never thought that Mr Charlie, or the colonial powers of any of the Commonwealth countries, would be capable of holding power over Africans for long. Slavery could not last forever. Then Woodville laughed:

> A laugh which became a tornado, a very small circle of competing wind spat out like cough-induced mucus from Woodville's mouth. Woodville had spat a laugh at the great house. You could hear Mr Charlie's furniture crying as the winds squeezed them in its wild gyrating dance; could hear the wood and stone collapse and see the nothing left but foundation of Mr Charlie's great house that he had built. Woodville had laughed the great house off its base.[15]

Mr Charlie disappeared, and now the great house was gone; it was "nothing but a dung heap."[16] The freed laborers would have to decide what they would do with their future in freedom. That decision is the focus of the novel; however, it is unclear why Woodville laughed Mr Charlie's house down as it was his project as well as Mr Charlie's. Mr Charlie had great respect for Woodville and looked at their work together as a cooperative project or "patent." He sometimes seemed to pronounce his overseer's name as "Wood will." Wood was important for every aspect of their work:

Wood posts and rafters held our huts together; wood was burnt for white lime to make the strong stone castle in which Mr Charlie lived; wood was burnt for coal to iron clothes, cook and bake and a whole lot of it was needed in the boiling house to turn the cane juice into sugar crystals, so "wood" was really key to Mr Charlie.[17]

Brodber refrains from letting the reader know Woodville's real significance until the final chapters. She decides to make it a mystery, as befits Afrofuturism. The novel is about Black life after slavery and is, as Broadnax explains, full of historical references and mysterious shifts in time and space.[18]

Brodber is developing her fable of origins as well as discussing historical facts of slavery and its abolition in the British Commonwealth. Significantly, *The Rainmaker's Mistake* was published in 2007, marking the bicentennial of the 1807 act that "made it illegal for British subjects to buy or sell slaves"[19] and to ship them from Africa to the New World. Nevertheless, slave ships continued to bring enslaved persons to the West, particularly to the Caribbean islands, Brazil, and the United States. Even when British slave traders were arrested for piracy, the slave trade continued with the help of British ships and ports. The Abolition of Slavery Act was finally passed in London in 1833, and "on Aug. 1, 1834, all slaves six years old and younger were freed, but all older slaves moved into an apprentice cycle to be freed in four or more years."[20] Those "six years old and younger" would have included Queenie and the other children about to become members of "the pickney gang."

In 1838, enslaved persons were officially freed, according to the British Parliament's Emancipation Act. While Brodber is developing an imaginative fable, she also includes history. Fiction and history are important to all her novels. The close relationship between history and literature is discussed by Edouard Glissant, who writes that "History (whether we see it as expression or lived reality) and Literature form part of the same problematics."[21]

The first narrator, Queenie, is one of the seven (eight, if you count the twins as two) children who were not quite six years old and not yet a part of the "pickney gang" when Mr Charlie announced freedom for those enslaved. Queenie does not identify herself until nearly the middle of the novel, which increases the mystery. After the emancipation and the disappearance of Mr Charlie, his great house, the long table of the Last Supper, and the Edenic experience, Queenie introduces the rest of the island. She says that there are three "continents," separated by rivers:

> Here we were in the garden of Eden, every material need met, and we were standing still, dumbfounded. . . . So constantly did it [the water from the river] flow that it made small rivers separating us—Woodville on one side, I-Sis and Sallywater on the other, and the rest of us in-between. Three separate continents. Three sides of each washed by water, the fourth connected to our past.[22]

After emancipation, Queenie explains that since no one is weeding the fields anymore, she and her friends are tormented by ticks and lice, and members of the almost pickney gang begin to swim away from their original home "towards the unknown." They land on Cabarita Island, and some of the older generations soon follow them, including the caretakers who guided them as children—Miss Mathilde, Luke, and London. Other members of the older generation return to the yam area behind Mr Charlie's house (the place of the past), and later they bring dirt to extend the Cabarita Island and to grow more crops, such as cassava, bananas, pineapples, and vegetables. The older folks do not find cattle at Mr Charlie's. Nevertheless, after emancipation, Cabarita Island becomes the center for both the younger and older generations of the newly free. The island is separated from the past and allows the young generation more freedom to think for themselves.

While the youth feel that they are moving into the unknown, the older ones bring rules of the past and institution-building. They form councils to handle the business of living and tell the children that they need to go to school, but for this education, they will need a birth certificate and full name. Everyone knows this information would be impossible if they are really Mr Charlie's yam children, for no one knows their parents. As the older folks convene and make plans, a member of the younger generation, Essex, while playing a game with his friend Juba, falls off the side of the Cabarita Island into the sea, "between our island and the future, the unknown,"[23] and is away for a while. Later Essex will return in a flying sea machine that he has made himself. His building the flying sea plane is an example of the almost pickney gang's creativity, which defines them. They may have once thought they were yam people, good only for labor, but once they are free, they know they will find their true identities and their purpose.

The novel's landscape is separated by place, but also by time, and the reader finds that the plantation's formerly enslaved people must leave Cabarita Island from time to time to find out what the past was all about and what "the free" offers. But they cannot manage to raise enough crops, and they have no livestock to eat. In his seaplane, Essex flies somewhere between the past and Cabarita Island. He feels psychologically forced to find the knowledge of the distant past.[24] Later he is joined by Little Congo. The two of them bring food from the past to their friends and family on Cabarita Island. On Woodville's island (their old home on Mr Charlie's plantation), the birds with their various colors and voices lead them to find strange mounds in Woodville's area of the plantation, mounds of women that Woodville had loved and impregnated in the past—Jubbah, Phibbah, and Princess. These discoveries are apparently mounds of the mothers of the children who were said to have been born of yams and to have come to be the enslaved persons of Mr Charlie. Ultimately, Essex and Little Congo arrange to bring back crops and livestock to the people of Cabarita Island from the past.

Such shifts of time and space in *The Rainmaker's Mistake* reflect the fantasy of magical realism, speculative fiction, and Afrofuturism, as defined by Kelly Josephs and Mark Dery.[25] The reader must accept the gaps in time and space in Brodber's novel so that the narrative can continue moving forward, but the characters are constantly moving through time and space so that they can come to understand their true identities. According to Josephs, this fluidity of time and space is a feature of the novel, as it is in most of Brodber's fiction. While the novel's characters are sometimes on Cabarita Island, the young people, especially the almost pickney clan, and the elders who follow them, are in a later time and place—the present, or "the Norm." Additionally, as

Josephs points out, "we later learn that there is the Future, where one of the Cabarita residents, London, travels via a mysterious seaway to trade produce for manufactured goods."[26] London (who was Abdul in the African past) decides that he should visit the future also to sell some of their produce—bananas, coconuts, plantains—and to buy clothes, plates, and lamps. He would learn more about the ways of the people of the future as well. Luke (also an elder spirit) watches out for movements on the beaches to protect those inhabitants of Cabarita Island and to look out for Mr Charlie. London knows that the youth need to go to school, even if they could not find their birth certificates. They never could find their father, but one day they do find Woodville, "a dried-up piece of sawdust lying on the beach."[27] They use feathers to see if Woodville is alive.

By this point in the novel, Queenie, who has been revealed as the main narrator, has also left Cabarita Island to visit I-Sis and Sallywater's part of the island. But there she finds a different world where people age, die, and are buried. To her horror, Sallywater, once her age, is an old woman, and Sallywater's mother, I-Sis, has died. During one of Queenie's visits, Sallywater also dies and is buried. According to Queenie:

> The older smiling sister who said she was Sallywater, the one who had been engaging me, been waiting for the chance to laugh at me (it seemed), the whisper of the Sallywater that I knew, with stretched skin gathered at the corner of her eyes, the unlit pipe between her gums on which she now and again sucked, fingers sheer bones holding a stick, said:—Hush,—to the speaker, still unintroduced. And the two sisters [Sallywater and Queenie], images of I-Sis and Sallywater smiled at each other.[28]

Since I-Sis had died by this time, Sallywater and Queenie act like sisters and plot what they will do now to make sense of things, now that they are free.

From these former associates, Queenie finds out—first from Sallywater—that being born into slavery had stunted them, and they had been told many lies, such as that they were born from yams.

They had not aged while they were enslaved and were not awake to their surroundings. However, when Woodville reappears to them on Cabarita Island, he is just a slug of what he had been and seems near death, but he hangs on and makes their lives miserable with the constant demand of care. Woodville is only a remnant from the past, the voice of the colonial power, a skeleton of another time.

Sallywater awakens Queenie to much that she suffered at the hands of Mr Charlie and Woodville during colonial times. I-Sis and Sallywater had always remained aware of the blinding system, and I-Sis knew that her daughter was the product of her union with Woodville, a liaison that she called off after the child's birth or "outdooring."[29] Since then, Sallywater, the daughter, has grown up and had children, and her children and grandchildren had produced children. Unlike I-Sis, Sallywater cannot explain the yam story, but she knows that somehow Mr Charlie and Woodville had marked the laborers so that they would not grow old, and the owners of the plantation would not have to train new laborers or confront resistance.

After sharing much of the past with Queenie and introducing her to her granddaughter's daughter, Janique, who seems to be about Queenie's age, Sallywater dies and is rolled into a cloth and buried by the people of the community. Queenie leaves with Janique to go to a university (in "the Norm," or the present, perhaps in North America), where she learns about loving, sexuality, and "naturalness." She even engages in an affair with Janique's boyfriend because she does not understand love and jealousy until she is guilty of both. Queenie eventually earns an MD and a degree in anthropology. She then returns to Cabarita Island as a healer and uses the medical arts learned during her studies in the "Norm," the Eurocentric and scientific world of the present.

Queenie, Essex, and Little Congo must go back to their past before they can enter the future. However, Jupiter has been "sucked into the Future," but nobody talks about him, we presume because of his unhappy circumstances after leaving the world of Cabarita Island.[30] Jupiter, one of Queenie's cohorts, had been miserable on Cabarita Island. Unlike the others who had been injected by a chemical in the neck or under the chin by Mr Charlie or Woodville, to prevent further maturation, Jupiter had grown and aged. He first noticed age when his penis began to grow without stopping. His older brother, London, takes him to the city, where he visits a prostitute and learns about sex and growth. Eventually, he travels to the future, away from Cabarita Island, probably to the United States, where he must accept his life of growth, but unfortunately, he ends up in prison, instead of in the wide-open spaces of his homeland.

Unlike Jupiter, however, Queenie, Essex, and Little Congo return to Cabarita Island just in time to see Woodville as he is dying. The three time-travelers show him the mound markers for Princess, Phibbah, and Jubbah. Woodville cries, and Queenie thinks that it is because of his love for these women. They bury Woodville with the mound markers of what they assume to be his three wives. His death marks the end of the false myth that they had been brought up with, the most outrageous of the many myths that deceived the enslaved laborers of Mr Charlie and made them think they were yams, not the human productions of the slaveholder and the overseer. Woodville dies with a smile on his face; he is smiling at Queenie because she knows most of the long history of the community, even their lives in Africa.

London, whose African ancestral spirit was Abdul, tells Queenie that Woodville smiled because he knew that Queenie would eventually discover why Mr Charlie's laborers were brought from Africa to the Americas. Eager to learn the whole truth of the past, Queenie hypnotizes London, so that she can address his spirit Abdul in her time. Central to those truths, Queenie discovers that Woodville is the rainmaker of the title, who made the serious mistake of sending the rains.[31] When Queenie hypnotizes London after Woodville's death, he fulfills Woodville's final request: "Abdul [London], tells the children. Guide them. Kofi (or Luke) will help as usual."[32] Woodville also repeats a poetic line by the British poet Alfred, Lord Tennyson: "Who has seen her wave her hand / or o'er the casement stand?" He seems to be referring to I-Sis and Sallywater. Later we learn that I-Sis was Abdul's (London's) sister, and he could not leave her, although he was about to do so when he followed Woodville (the African spirit Tayeb) away from Africa to the Americas.

Woodville, or Tayeb, had told London, or Abdul, that he believed what "the men in the white jackets" had told him about the new world, and he colluded with them in Africa (whom he calls Mother) and decided to go travel with them to the unknown people. They injected him with some amnesiac drug, and he let them take his people to the Americas. Presumably, he was responsible for letting the Europeans seize and enslave many of his people. He intended to bring the rain to help them all to find the unknown new world and fulfill their dreams and curiosity, but the rains only moved the ships faster and more effectively separated them from their Mother Africa.

In addition, the rains made them lose all memories of the world they had known, completely divorcing them from their past. In a sense, Woodville (Tayeb) had committed matricide or "Genosuicide" (a word coined by Erna Brodber).[33] Woodville had helped the Europeans take the Africans from Africa, and the rains had washed away much of their knowledge of their mother and home. Tayeb, or Woodville, had helped to deplete Mother Africa: "The rains came. . . . They showed us our mother's body swept away by the tide of Tayeb's rains. . . . He had committed matricide."[34] This misjudgment was "the rainmaker's mistake." Woodside had believed that the Africans (his brothers) would find a better life in America. He had even compounded his mistake by making the rains come and sending the slave ships more quickly to the Americas.

In Jamaica, their new world, Tayeb's friends—Abdul/London, Kofi/Luke, Mathilde, and I-Sis—were no longer themselves. Woodville, or Tayeb, continues his collusion with Mr Charlie in the development of his plantations. Woodville oversees his friends and their descendants as enslaved laborers, whom Mr Charlie needs to develop the crops and the livestock that made the patent a vast business enterprise. It prospered until the emancipation of enslaved persons, when Tayeb/Woodville, the rainmaker, once again blew his horn ("the kaachi"), as he had in Africa when the Africans were kidnapped:

> My sound was a river cutting the earth, bounding off the boulders it exposed, running with dear life through grasslessness, treelessness, so I gave in Man. I let them take us, Abdul. I let the white coats take us, inject us—says this poor brother, Tayeb, my brother, the rainmaker, sheets of water flowing over and over the bridge of his nose, flowing through the sinuses of his ears. Those were whey-faced holy ghosts, they had broken the brother.[35]

When Woodville dies and is buried, the younger generation of those Africans who had been brought to the world across the Atlantic have worked to find out their new mission and have looked to the future as well as to the far past. When the emancipated people discover their true history and their mission, they begin to move forward, as Queenie and Essex do when they find that they can marry. They have a child, with the knowledge of their "naturalness," mortality, and hope. Their plan is to start a new nation free of Mr Charlie, who is rotting in a cave below the ground, and Woodville, who is buried below those grounds as well. They will fashion this new world together "in the free."[36]

NOTHING'S MAT AND THE ART OF FRACTALS AND ANCESTRY

Like *The Rainmaker's Mistake*, Brodber's fifth novel, *Nothing's Mat*, published by the University of the West Indies Press in 2014, is a novel of the continuing generations—the new African Jamaican diaspora or what Velma Pollard calls "tomorrow's spaces." The novel has multiple narrators, but primarily Princess, a young woman of Jamaican ancestry who has grown up with her parents in London. The characters are all members of or related to a Jamaican family. They also have family members in the United States, the United Kingdom, and Panama in Central and South America. In other words, they are all a part of the African diaspora. The author also concentrates on the idea of fractals, which are infinitely complex patterns that are similar across different scales.[37] Like fractals, the family has grown up with a repeating pattern of races and ethnicities.

The novel is both historical and speculative. It begins spiritually as early as the beginning of the Atlantic slave trade and the movement of African indentured servants to Jamaica. The character Modibe, a member of a family of indentured servants, is killed during the Morant Bay Rebellion of 1865, and Maud, his would-be girlfriend, is raped by British soldiers. While the rebellion is discussed briefly in the first part of the novel, the historical event is more fully discussed in the second part. *Nothing's Mat* is also speculative, and some of the characters are repeated in future generations; for example, "Modibe the second" and "Clarise the second" are born to members of the family in the novel's third generation, which is described in the final section. Because of the interplay of past and present, spirituality and historicity, the book often seems more speculative or Afrofuturist than realistic.[38]

Nothing's Mat consists of three main parts. Although each has a distinctive function within the novel's structure, all three parts include shifts in time and space, as also seen in *The Rainmaker's Mistake* and other speculative and Afrofuturistic fiction.

Part One

In this opening part of the novel, the narrator introduces all the main characters, including herself, whose name is Princess, and her parents, Herbert and Grace, who have Jamaican ancestry but live in London. Princess is the narrator in the beginning and for much of the novel. She grows up in England, and while she is in sixth form, the final level of secondary education in British and Commonwealth schools, she decides to write a long paper instead of "sitting a formal exam."[39] Her father suggests that she research a history of his Jamaican family and fill in the many gaps that he grew up with. Her mother agrees that her husband's family is full of incredulity and gaps and suggests that Princess should work on discovering the genealogy of Cousin Nothing, who is supposed to be the sister of her father's mother, Pearl, but is not really his mother's sister at all. Princess's father suggests that she travel to Jamaica to visit his parents and raise pertinent questions. His parents are in their late eighties, and Princess's questions should be asked before it is too late.

Princess meets Cousin Nothing, also known as Conut, for the first time at seventeen, while she studies her father's family in Jamaica. Conut is thirty years of age, and she loves singing and holding on to her knowledge of family and traditions. But she has a habit of physically falling or fainting and calling Princess's grandparents for help. Her telegram for assistance comes when Princess is visiting Jamaica. Princess goes to stay with Conut and runs errands for her. Princess lives in her own state of "nothingness" because she has never been able to find her identity in England. She says to herself, "Now in my feeling of nothingness, I look in the skies and there is Cousin Nothing [Conut] like Mary Poppins floating in the skies on her sisal mat."[40] Princess believes that Conut's knowledge of her family history gives her cousin strength, and it will give her the strength that she needs as well.

Princess and Conut become friends. Conut says that she herself could not eat vegetables, particularly the vegetable dasheen, which is a version of callaloo. The next morning Princess finds out why. While she and Conut are walking in the garden, Princess sees a very human-like dasheen, a plant with elephant ears, a perennial plant native to West Africa. Conut calls the dasheen "Keith" and later shares a story with Princess. A friend was on her deathbed when she told Conut the story of her pregnancy. The friend said that when she was pregnant, she and her lover discovered that the farm owner, Mass Eustace, had poisoned his plants to keep people from stealing them. Conut's friend had a baby that was half-human and half-dasheen.

Conut had an affection for the baby dasheen, named Keith. When the mother died, Conut put Keith in a little house in the bush. The dasheen plant and human together was an example of fractal art: that is, the plant was a natural phenomenon that exhibited a repeated pattern at different levels.[41] The story of Keith is also a traditional African story. According to Princess, the dasheen plant was also called the "ping-wing macca," the subject of her father's favorite song, "*Mi heng it pon ping wing macca*," which represents "the natural path" of the family history.[42] She explains:

> One leaf would emerge, then another, then two—the sum of one and one—then three—the sum of two and one—then three—the sum of two and one . . . and so on, the number of leaves continuing to determine the next number of leaves to infinity.[43]

During another one of their walks, Conut and Princess chop down a dasheen plant, take out the stringy interior, and wash and hang the strings. With the fibers known as sisal, Conut and Princess begin to make "never-ending circles and string together a mat of family" or a family tree mat.[44] Ultimately, Princess earns an A on her long paper about the family history and learns so many family secrets that she begins to understand her own identity. At the end of Princess's paper, the teacher writes that literature often speaks of the West Indian family as "fractured," but that Princess might be able to prove it was a fractal.[45]

In "Patterns of Loving: Erna Brodber's *Nothing's Mat*," Romdhani describes the next chapter about the untimely and disturbing rape of the young teenager, Clarise (Conut's mother): "One of the main themes in the following section, as is the case in Brodber's earlier novel *Jane and Louisa Will Soon Come Home* (1980), is the consequence of female sexuality being taboo."[46] Clarise, who is still in puberty, is raped by the neighbor, Mass Eustace, when she had been "playing house" with her friend Neville in Mass Eustace's garden. Mass Eustace says he will tell Maud, Clarise's sister and guardian, as well as the pastor, who will put her and Neville out of the Christian Endeavor group. He then takes Clarise and puts her legs around his waist and rapes her. She is naïve and does not know what happened until she gives birth to a baby in the latrine and is caught by Maud. Maud and Clarise name the baby Nothing because they think they can get nothing from Mass Eustace. However, something about the child reminds Mass Eustace of his mother. His sister, Euphemie, from Panama, thinks so, too, and tells her brother that he should marry Clarise. However, Clarise becomes ill with consumption and soon dies. As a result, Mass Eustace marries Maud instead.

Much later, Neville, the former friend of Clarise, shows up at Mass Eustace's estate to see the child. However, Pearl (Princess's grandmother) marries Neville. He is a successful teacher, and Pearl helps him have a beautiful home and family. One of their children is Herbert, who becomes a lawyer in England. Herbert marries a foundling, Grace, who, unlike her husband, has no knowledge of her family. Their child is Princess, whose study of the family and meeting with her cousin Nothing/Conut leads to the plot of the novel.

Part Two

In the second part of the novel, Princess elaborates upon various characters and episodes already mentioned in Part One. Her circles on the mat clarify much of the first part and give historical context to the actions. When Princess returns to Jamaica, she is thirty years of age and plans to find out more details of her family ancestry while working on her MA and PhD at the University of the West Indies at Mona in Kingston, Jamaica. After her cousin dies, along with the dasheen Keith, Princess decides to continue working on "Nothing's mat" and to add important events and persons who also participated in the family's development.

In this part, the narrator often becomes Maud, from St. Thomas Parish, who is raped by British soldiers during the Morant Bay Rebellion. Maud describes the past in detail, beginning with a narration of the rebellion, which occurred in St. Thomas Parish, Jamaica, in 1865.[47] In Part One, the narrator Princess had described how Maud and Clarise, the younger sister of Modibe (one of the indentured servants who was killed during the rebellion), traveled from St. Thomas to St. Mary Parish to get away from the British soldiers.

Princess again becomes the narrator temporarily and describes how Maud and Clarise (who will become the mother of Conut) meet and how they enter the community of African Jamaican history. Maud and Clarise were both originally from Stony Gut, Jamaica, in St. Thomas Parish, which was walking distance from Morant Bay. Brodber takes this opportunity to present her historiography of the rebellion that took place in Morant Bay in 1865, when newly freed Black people and Black indentured servants fought against the British colonial government to establish their judicial rights and to buy more property on the island. The narrator shifts back to Maud, who is only sixteen years old at the time, but feels compassion for one of the young African indentured servants, Modibe, who is often at the bay with his family. According to Maud, "They had come on contract and could get a piece of land when they finished their five years [of servitude]."[48] But even though these indentured servants could acquire property by law, they were often cheated out of much of their land. Brodber makes the most of this opportunity to stress that much injustice occurred on the colonial island even after slavery was abolished.

Injustice persisted in the court system at Morant Bay. The narrator describes a court case that is occurring at the time. A young man, at the age of sixteen, is told that he is penalized four shillings, but in this case, he must pay four times that much—sixteen sixpence. Maud's cousin, Daddy B, cries out that he must pay only the four shillings. Even though the court officers put him out of the courthouse, he continues to call out, "4 shillings." The policemen soon come out to Stoney Gut to notify Daddy B that he must come back to court and make his statement again. Several policemen march him to Morant Bay with their guns, but surprisingly Maud comes to the court also with a crowd of others to defend Daddy B. The women go to the court first. They take off their skirts and wear only their petticoats. Led by Maud, they start a fire in the courthouse. The indentured servants march down the road. The young man who leads them is Modibe, Maud's friend. He and the rest of the men come out with their cutlasses to confront the police officers. Maud, the narrator now, describes the scene, using the Jamaican Creole language:

> Then my whole world turn upside down for who was coming down the road happy as pappy with a set of his people from a side road, but Modibe. Dem Africans have a way of running like dem going to fall on them face . . . ; coming down and it pretty so 'til and is my Modibe leading them. He wave his cutlass in the air but that is how dem do when dem happy. He is shouting something that sound like Manalva, but I know it is "Nana Reba" he say, for he confirms it to me. It means "the Queen is coming." His eyes lock on me and I feel like today is the day when our two families going to do the joining.[49]

The reader has learned in Part One that Maud started a fire when the police came to the courthouse. Maud and other women ignite the fire to end the battle. Maud says in Jamaican Creole, "I take the lady's fire stick and other people join in, some ah blow fire and some ah put coconut coir pon it to make the fire come up fast."[50] Maud's father comes to take her away from the battle. But the officers kill Modibe and many of the other participants. Maud leads the funeral dance, but officers stop the funeral procession and rape Maud, right in front of her father. The father and mother tell Maud that, although she has pain from the brutal rape, she must take Modibe's little sister, Clarise, whom the police would also kill, and walk all the way to St. Mary Parish, where they will escape from the officers and finally find peace.

The second part of the book is about their long journey and the little girl Clarise's growing up.

Maud and Clarise walk along "like the children of Israel through the wilderness."[51] They work well together, except that Clarise continues to look at men, thinking that one of them might be her father or her brother Modibe, although she had heard that all the people of her home, Stony Gut, had been killed by the officers. Clarise is also almost attacked by a Chinese man in the Barbican, and Maud hits the man, then tells Clarise that she is acting like "a alabaster dolly baby what backra pickney play with."[52] Sometimes Maud pretends to be Clarise's sister, but she usually acts more like her mother. Clarise's naiveté on the walk from Morant Bay to St. Mary Parish foreshadows her being molested by Mass Eustace, the fifty-year-old neighbor of Maud and Clarise.

Part Three

While the second part of the novel delved into the past and was told from multiple points of view, the fractal pattern takes another turn in this final part, which is narrated by Princess and her cousin Joy. The plot begins to emphasize Princess's interactions with the younger generation of the family in the United States. Princess's father, Herbert, has kept up with his half-brother, John, and half-sister, Sally, who are the children of Herbert's mother, Pearl, from an earlier marriage to a "silver" (biracial) man from the US, who worked on building the Panama Canal. Joy is one of John's children, who live in the US. She teaches at Howard University, is very race-conscious, and takes part in the civil rights and Black Power movements, but her sister Grace is decidedly apolitical and marries "Old Tom," who perpetuates a low idea of Black people.

In this part, the family of Princess expands. There is much repetition, or recursion, in the family. Joy leaves the United States and travels to Jamaica to meet several members of her family and to give birth to her child as an unmarried woman. She plans to have her baby at Princess's house in rural Jamaica, in the former house of Nothing/ Conut. It is the house that Cousin Nothing willed to Princess upon her death. Joy and Princess become close friends and work together to complete the family mat. Joy wants her child to be born in rural Jamaica, to register the baby to her cousin Princess, and to pretend that it is Princess's child. Joy will then adopt the child before she returns home to the US, where she will raise her child without shame. She names her child "Modibe the second." Surprisingly, Princess has a child at the same time as Joy, making the cousins' maternity simpatico.

Princess ends up marrying Joy's doctor and gives birth to another child, "Clarise the second," even though the doctor says that she is perimenopausal. For the birth and naming of Princess's second child, Princess and Joy and their husbands all come to Princess's home. Finally, Princess learns that Joy's lover and the father of her child was biracial like Pearl's first husband. Joy later makes her own family mat and includes the American connections. Princess is happy that the children all know each other and emanate "happy energy." Junior, the doctor, says, "Another set of recursions and iterations."

Princess reflects:

> They won't know the nothingness that set me to completing Nothing's mat, because they understand more about ancestral spirits and energy than I knew at thirty. I do feel that I have accomplished something: I have set them off on the right path.[53]

In both *The Rainmaker's Mistake* and *Nothing's Mat*, the protagonists move to finding their way "in the free." They find out how they fit into the family and the community and how to fulfill themselves in the future. In *Nothing's Mat*, the making of the family mat helps all members of the family discover how they came into the world and what is expected of them. Younger family members plan to make, or add to, the mat themselves so that they can include themselves and more of the family that they know well. In *The Rainmaker's Mistake*, the newly freed people realize that they must seek their place in the world during the age of postcolonialism in the present and the future, although they must also remember the past.

Chapter 6

GENDER AND IDENTITY IN THE SHORT FICTION OF VELMA POLLARD AND ERNA BRODBER

Erna Brodber and Velma Pollard have always written short stories while also writing novels and poetry. They both began with short fiction, and their most recent books are collections of their stories. These volumes are Pollard's *Considering Woman I & II: New and Selected Stories* (2011) and Brodber's *The World Is a High Hill* (2012). The stories feature Jamaican women as they struggle against a patriarchal society, which has led to many gaps in gender equality in education, employment, and social development. In the stories, as Nain and Bailey point out, the women characters search for their identities and place in the community.[1] Based on the sisters' own experiences as diasporic women, their personal stories are also stories of Jamaican culture and myth. Their short fiction provides examples of Brodber and Pollard's overall themes of migration, gender, history, and resistance.

In their fiction, the sisters demonstrate the oppressions that women and girls have historically suffered in Jamaica as in much of the world. There are gaps between the expectations of boys and girls as they grow up, as well as in their educational ventures, employment and salaries, and political achievements, even though gaps between the lives and expectations of men and women in Jamaica have decreased dramatically in the late twentieth and early twenty-first centuries.[2] For instance, more girls and women are attending schools and universities today; Jamaica has elected a woman prime minister and mayor of Kingston; and women are filling some of the highest-paying jobs. But there is still a large discrepancy between what most women and men earn in their employment, and many women still hold jobs as domestics or helpers. Brodber's and Pollard's short fiction pushes back against these circumscribed roles in a compelling way. After discussing these themes in both women's stories, I end this chapter with some concluding thoughts on my experience with their work.

VELMA POLLARD'S SHORT FICTION

Pollard has three collections of short stories: *Considering Woman*, published in 1989; *Karl and Other Stories*, published in 1994, and *Considering Woman I & II*, published in 2010.[3] *Considering Woman* begins with sections titled "Parables" and "Cages" about the constrictions placed upon women, particularly women artists, in married life. In the first poetic epigraph to the volume, "Women Poets (with your permission)," the woman poet-speaker conceals her writing from her husband, but he looks at the poem anyway and makes corrections while complimenting her and her friends for taking up such a difficult task. The second epigraph, "Version," is based on Genesis, with the married couple being Adam and Eve. Eve hides her writing under her fig leaf. The husband is not angry in either poem, but he is patriarchal and condescending about what he considers his wife's foolish literary attempts.

The same type of hiding and trying to find her identity as a working woman and writer occurs in all three stories in the section "Cages." In the story "Cage II," a woman leaves her husband, and a colleague proposes to marry her. However, she is enjoying her freedom so much that she says to her mother: "Listen Mummy, I have a feeling this generation of men and women can't make it. This generation of women asking for bread and the men offering crumbs. Now women can feed, house, clothe themselves, and are looking for something more."[4] From her own experience, Pollard writes several stories about the patriarchy of much of Jamaican society, particularly in rural areas.

In her more recent volume of stories, *Considering Woman I and II*, Pollard continues to deal with Jamaican discrimination against women in terms of sexuality and marriage and attitudes of discrimination due to class and color. She also uses inventive styles of narration that include various points of view, such as first-person observers, multiple perspectives, and matters of historiography. For example, the story "Orinthia, Is That You?" has several perspectives. The narrative time is August 1, and the First of August Fair is taking place as the day regarded in Jamaica as Emancipation and Liberation Day. The emancipation of enslaved persons in all British Commonwealth countries was announced on August 1, 1838. However, Liberation Day also commemorated the liberation of the colony of Jamaica from Great Britain.[5]

The narrator of "Orinthia, Is That You?" begins by saying, "That time Emancipation Day was big. That time we were still one people glad for freedom, not yet out of many one." "Out of many one" became the Jamaica motto after its independence occurred in 1962. The Jamaican people accepted that they were mostly of African descent, but there were many other ethnicities. The motto assured capitalists that Jamaica would not become a communist country like Cuba. The slogan conveyed that the poor would not rebel against the oppression that they suffered due to the economy but would still have hope that all classes and ethnicities would work together. The many groups—Indians, Chinese, Africans, and Europeans, rich and poor, young and old—would prosper together. That ideology was a major theme of post-independence political thought.[6]

In the story, J. G. Dewberry, sometimes called Jewbarry, dressed elegantly in his "cutaway suit, gold chain leading into his pocket watch," is walking along at the fair.[7] He has just returned to Jamaica from the United States, where he had gone to receive a fellowship to attend medical school and become a doctor. But he never became a doctor. He has become a taxi driver and is transporting people around in his cart at the fair. Reflecting on the past and his childhood with his grandmother, he remembers going to fairs and eating ice cream, mango shakes, and various Jamaican foods, such as curried goat, which he orders from a booth in the fair. Dewberry looks at the booth owner and is surprised when he recognizes a woman from the past. He says in wonder, "Is that you, Orinthia?" And she responds, "Is that you, George Jewbarry?"[8] What, after all, is the man's name? Is it Dewberry or Jewbarry? It is probably Dewberry, but the young man had changed it to Jewbarry to make it, he thought, more appropriate for living and achieving something in New York City.

The story becomes more complex when Dewberry remembers fifteen years earlier when he was twenty years of age, and the booth owner was only sixteen and a helper in the well-to-do Georges' household. Then he first met Orinthia and had sex with her immediately in the Georges' kitchen. The young Dewberry often went to get his lunch there while he was attending secondary school nearby. He regretted when he found out that she had become pregnant because of their encounters in the Georges' house. There was nothing he could do because he was ambitious, and he had already made plans to leave for medical school in the United States. The young woman wants Dewberry to know that she had married a carpenter and that he should meet his daughter, who is also present at the fair. The father looks her over. He sees that she is very pretty like her mother, and his blood rushes to the roots of his hair. Orinthia feels that although she had initially disappointed her mother and grandmother, she had gone on to do well for herself and her daughter and had even started her own business. The reader realizes that Orinthia has accomplished as much or more than George Dewberry, the man she once loved.

"Orinthia, Is That You?" is a typical story in *Considering Woman I & II*. The oppression of Jamaican women, particularly due to class and patriarchal customs, is the subject of most of the stories. The tales are often told by a narrator who is from the rural area and is observing social situations and commenting on the injustices toward women. Pollard has gathered three groups of tales in *Considering Woman I & II*. "Orinthia, Is That You?" belongs to the first group, called "Bitter Tales." They all relate to the hypocrisy of many men and their patriarchal ways of interacting with women. The second group of tales is called "On My Way to Somewhere, Of Course." These tales depict similar patterns of male patriarchy in other islands of the Caribbean.

In Pollard's first volume of short stories, *Considering Woman*, she writes about dislocation. The displacement felt by many women from the Caribbean and Africa who have migrated to New York City is the subject of many stories. "Sister I" (one of two "Sister" stories) portrays a North African woman who jumps with her children from an upper floor apartment window in a well-to-do area of Manhattan. A taxi driver notices the light of three swift arcs from a balcony of the apartment building. On the street below, a security woman in orange overalls, who helps children cross the streets, is shocked when she sees the "children's twisted faces [as they fall]. And the agonized stare in a young woman's face. All three bodies lie broken on the pavement."[9] The United Nations (UN) ladies at their tea that day watch televised news shows and talk about the young woman, whose husband works on UN committees. She killed herself and her two children because of her feelings of loneliness and dislocation.

"My Mother (for Marjorie)" is another story of migration and loss, narrated by a daughter who, like her mother, has left Jamaica to move to New York City. The narrator describes all the frightened, tense people getting off the subway. She imagines her mother doing the same. She then remembers the trips that she and her grandmother had taken in the past to the bus station in rural Jamaica to pick up the boxes her mother had sent regularly from the United States to Jamaica, and she recalls the clothes that did not really fit but she wore with pride to Sunday concerts and other social events. She remembers her grandmother's lectures that she must show gratitude and write thank-you letters to her mother.

Despite her mother's many promises, the daughter says that her mother never had the money to return to Jamaica and visit her daughter and other relatives, but one day her mother's coffin came home instead: "The coffin was foreign—large, heavy, silvery, straight from the USA. The woman in the coffin was not my mother."[10] Many community people left big gaudy wreaths on her mother's grave, but she left her "maiden-hair fern," which continued to grow as the years passed.[11] She did not cry at the funeral, but she does cry on 14th Street in Manhattan upon arriving there and seeing the many women in their wigs, rushing to work, as she imagines her mother did. She knows that her mother had never known the peace of the Jamaican countryside that she had felt as she and her grandmother had traveled to the bank to pick up wires and boxes from her mother. But she was sure that "the maiden-hair fern was still lush" on her mother's grave as a maidenhair fern adds nobility and beauty to a grave and its inhabitant.[12]

The desolation but urgent longing to "go up" to the United States is described in the story "Georgia and Them There United States" in the collection *Karl and Other Stories*.[13] The narrator, June, feels sorry for her Aunt Teach (Leticia) because of her aunt's loneliness in an American city. June remembers the way she and her friends in Jamaica had always thought that the clothes, cards, and shoes sent from America were the finest products: "I wrote home to my father and begged him not to tell anybody I had gone UP to the United States."[14] She felt ashamed of her migration, presumably because she had left her homeland for what she thought would be better employment and educational opportunities.

Pollard's tales of marriage are often unhappy. Although there are many variations, most of them take place in the countryside, particularly in *Karl and Other Stories*, but the women are always marginalized and, as the individuals Spivak calls the "subalterns," they usually cannot speak.[15] Such is the case with Betsy Hyde, Miss Chandra, and Miracle Linda in their tales. Dorlene, in "A Night's Tale," almost succumbs to losing her husband, Jacob, to the New Orleans woman who comes to their home in Jamaica to be with him, but with the help of her Muma, she discovers their affair. She puts a suitcase full of his clothes outside the house when Jacob returns home, saying, "Jacob gone five years now. And you know I never take another man."[16] Her husband's transgression causes Dorlene to give up on men.

Pollard's stories often treat the theme of marriage difficulties, particularly the marriages of women artists. In one of these stories, "Rainbow Corner," the protagonist is a musician dying of cancer. She has left her husband to live with a fellow musician, who is her soul mate. This man loves her for her humility and sensitivity. Now her first husband (her only husband really, for he is a Catholic and will not give her a divorce), as well as her grown children, come by to see her. Her lover also comes to the hospital to visit, but she asks her nurse to keep them all out when she becomes very feeble. The nurse puts a peephole in the corner so that her lover, Mr. Strom, can peep in to see her. She is almost disappearing, getting thinner and thinner, but she can hear her lover when he sings their favorite song: "I'm saving my money / To buy you a rainbow. . . . / After I've bought you a rainbow / I'll go out and buy you the moon."[17] Mr. Strom knows that she hears him: "He knew she was singing in her heart."[18] As Pollard explained in a 2008 article, the two lovers can only express their love through the song they both sing.[19]

In an interview with Daryl Cumber Dance, expert on the writings of both sister-writers, Pollard and fellow Jamaican writer Pamela Mordecai discussed the complex role that women writers often fill when they are married. As women, they are expected to put their husbands and their children first before their work. "Then you get a little moment," said Pollard; "certainly poetry is something you write, and you enjoy it and so, but you don't see yourself as a poet."[20] Pollard writes from her own bittersweet experience as a Caribbean woman.

Along with the stories called "Cages" in *Considering Woman*, Pollard wrote the poem "After Cages" in response to her feeling that wives often feel trapped by their circumstances.[21] "After Cages" apparently depicts a mother and father who live in rural Jamaica. In the words of the daughter, the father spends his time reading the Sunday paper and grunting, ignoring the mother, who looks out the window at the rain falling on the pebbles, but reminds him to call his mother. The daughter imagines her mother leaving her husband one day: "Someday I'd say / she'll up and go / leaving her window-peering silent / newly old." However, time has passed, and there is no need to leave now. The father has died; "no going when it's no one that you are leaving."[22] But in the last lines, we may also surmise that the mother has died as well: the mother was one of the "lonely women newly old / but oddly silenced now / Stretched out beside the flowers / boxed brown in aged mahogany."[23] The mother has withered away in a spiritual sense.

Pollard's collection *Considering Woman* ends with the third story of the section called "Tales of Mothering." "Gran," a story inspired by the maternal grandmother of Pollard and Brodber, paints an important portrait of the typical rural Jamaican woman who owns property and obtains the ability to take care of herself and her family. She is full of energy and confidence that her religious beliefs, family, and community will carry her through even difficult times. Pollard emphasizes this by including it in both her first collection of stories, *Considering Woman*, and her latest collection, *Considering Woman I & II*.[24] The story begins, "When we were little, remember, the world was full of pastures and pastures were full of cow-dung."[25] The narrator moves from the present to the past quickly, and times change dramatically. The story jumps to the end of the tale when the grandmother's home has been occupied by numerous squatters. In the oven-house:

> Swarthy old women, each with her long hair in a single braid, squatted near the ground each with her long hair in a single braid.... There were flies all over the floor.... The women were all creasing their foreheads, flat like dingy squares of off-white sugar paper . . . and moaning, "Craab, craab, craab."[26]

The filthy floors of the oven-house were covered with cane trash and flies. Sometimes the granddaughter would take a tin of biscuits downhill to the squatters, leave, and look back "as Lot's wife died and froze into my mind a new last picture of Comfort Hall."[27] When the granddaughter leaves, she sits on the bank and thinks she should never have visited. She should have just kept her old memories of Comfort Hall, her grandmother's home.

Pollard explained in an interview, "I decided to write about my grandmother because I loved her, but also because she represents one kind of Jamaican woman, the kind that is called the backbone of this country. I wanted people to know about this kind of woman."[28] Pollard truly admired her grandmother, fondly remembering her. She also wanted to describe the changes that have occurred in Jamaican history, an important theme in both Pollard's and Brodber's short fiction, poetry, and novels. Unlike current conditions, the grandmother's home and farm were once large and clean. Gran alone used the oven-house, and she loved to serve the grandchildren breakfast of buns and totos, pears, and tangerines. In "Gran," the narrator recites the nursery song that the grandchildren sang as they climbed the hill to Gran's house: "Children, children / Yes Mummah / Where have you been to? / Grand-mummah / What did she give you? / Bread and Pear."[29]

Gran had a reputation for Christian morality in the community; people thought that she had "a special telephone arrangement with God."[30] People listened to her because of this special connection. For example, Gran insisted that two people who wanted to move into her extra rooms with their two little girls must marry first. She made a down payment on a wedding ring for them, and Miss Mamma and Mass Nate "'turn thanks' [marry] in front of everybody."[31] Gran was a matriarch who appointed herself the arbitrator of family disputes.

Gran's husband was Corpie, who is mentioned in several fictional works of both Pollard and Brodber. Despite fighting in the Boer War, he still had seven children with Gran. Unfortunately, he died young. In this story, it is said that he was poisoned by a woman who felt that the land he bought should belong to her family instead of his.[32] However, Gran continued to talk with Corpie and seek his advice after his death. In the last part of the story, Gran grows old and becomes more and more dependent on the ones she loves. When the narrator's mother dies, Gran moves into the mother's home to help the father for a while, but it does not work well for long, so she returns alone to Comfort Hall.

"My final guilt-ridden visit to that great old lady dogged me through young womanhood to maturity," reflects the narrator, "years after she [the grandmother] had taken up residence in heaven running errands for her God."[33] The narrator could never stay long enough with her grandmother in her last years. Her own family and job called her. When she received the news of Gran's death, the narrator sadly observes, "I was doing my penance out in the land of whiteness and success."[34] Here the narrator registers her displacement as she grieves.

In "Gran," Pollard echoes the theme of spirit possession, which often comes at death, as also explored by Brodber in her novels *Myal* and *Louisiana*. The narrator of the story knows: "My grandmother had died years before, quietly, without telling anybody, she had taken her spirit, while she still possessed it, up into the clouds to her God and let them take the body where they would."[35]

ERNA BRODBER'S SHORT FICTION

Brodber's short stories, particularly those published in *The World Is a High Hill*,[36] concentrate on women's lives as well. However, those tales published earlier in Brodber's literary career, such as "One Bubby Susan" and "Sleeping's Beauty and the Prince Charming,"[37] are interdisciplinary and, as Callaghan explains, also deal with history, myth, allegory, and spirituality.[38]

"One Bubby Susan" (1989), one of Brodber's early stories, draws upon the folklore of the Tainos, or Arawaks, the Indian group that first inhabited the island of Jamaica. The anthropologist Lesley-Gail Atkinson explains how much the Tainos influenced the country of Jamaica, noting that the name of Jamaica was, in fact, a derivation of the name the Tainos gave the island.[39] They called it Xaymaca, she says, which meant "land abounding with spring," and later, the word "Jamaica" was translated as "land of wood and water." Here Brodber solemnly remembers the indigenous origins of Jamaica.

In "One Bubby Susan," the narrator notes that she first heard the story of the rock carving on the cave, which opened into both Westmoreland and St. Mary Parishes from the sociologist and anthropologist Frank Cundall. He tells a scientific or scribal tale of the wood carving. However, the narrator does not believe the truth of Cundall's story until she smells the flowers that grow in the region of Dryland near Woodside and hears the voice of Susan, the Arawak woman in the cave herself. Brodber writes primarily from Susan's voice conveyed to the narrator, who is a sociologist herself. Susan's body has left her imprint on the cave door, and she is revealing the story to this sociologist, who, like Brodber, listens carefully to the Arawak woman's voice. The narrator uses Jamaican Creole, which once would not have been accepted as the words of a sociologist or anthropologist. However, Brodber, like Zora Neale Hurston, describes historical or sociological events from an insider's perspective.[40] Susan is determined to escape the restrictions placed on her as an Arawak woman of the late fifteenth century. In Jamaican Creole language,[41] the narrator writes:

> Miss Sue say, time for her to get married and she never was to married. She did like fly through cave and talk to *rat-bat* and climb tree and talk to bird and so on. She never want plant no maize and beat up nothing into mortar. But of fact all this bammy that her people so proud bout never mean one thing to her. Too dry.[42]

The Arawak woman, Susan, is determined to break away from the restrictions of her society's ideas of womanhood, and most of all, she refuses to marry. She simply lives in seclusion in the cave, and occasionally she steps outside the cave to breathe fresh air. But a young man sees her and spreads the word that a deity lives in the cave, a duppy or a god. The Arawak people begin to go to the cave and ask her questions. Since she won't answer and is of no help, they decide to stone her to death, and they knock off one of her breasts. When she falls, they continue the stoning, until they are only stoning the outline of her body. Their disdain for a woman who attempts to break away from society's principles is severe.

Brodber's postcolonial story "Sleeping's Beauty and a Prince Charming" is a twentieth-century version of the European folktale of Sleeping Beauty. In Brodber's tale, the sleeping princess is a Black woman who is little more than a sound without a body, especially for the Black prince, named Charming, who hears but does not see her. When Sleeping sees a knight moving around nearby on his horse, she sees him as a blind Samson or Saul (characters in the Old Testament) because while he could hear her breathing and imagines her staring at him, he cannot see her. To him, she is bodiless. Helen Tiffin, an influential scholar of postcolonial literary studies, writes that though Charming can feel her eyes on him and can pick up her "heavy vibrations," he cannot see her because to him, there is nobody/no body. By the conclusion of the parable, however, this Samson has regained his sight; he can now see Black womanhood, though he cannot fully accept her corporeality and her surprising re-embodiment after centuries of erasure.[43]

Prince Charming seems so absorbed by the European idea of Sleeping Beauty that he cannot fully see the African Jamaican woman before him. But they do engage in mental conversations about the past as formerly enslaved persons and subjects of Britain. He tells her that, as a spirit, he has seen the Asantehene and the pharaohs' tombs of Egypt, even though he is still a knight in the present time.[44] Sleeping says that she has been remembering much of the present and past herself. She reflects, "I am hoping to be of some use when those seven miles of the Black Star Line (Marcus Garvey's Black nationalist project) appears on the harbor."[45] Strikingly, Sleeping invokes Black resistance. As in Afrofuturistic fiction, Charming and Sleeping are living in both the past and the present, and they cannot come together corporeally, although they have a sense of each other's presence.

More recently, Rebecca Romdhani has written about the feelings, or affect, of the two characters, Sleeping and Charming, and their relationship with the dead.[46] As in most of Brodber's novels, the woman is just beginning to feel her sense of sexuality. Before her seven years of sleep, Sleeping had been consumed by her intellectual life. Now, although she is very eager to meet Charming, share her feelings with him, and perhaps be with him for the rest of her life, they are unable to unite. They remain so lost in their social roles as subjects of the United Kingdom and as members of a drastically patriarchal society that they cannot relax and be themselves, at one with their own identities. The story ends with the words, "*Rastafari me nuh chose none,*" which means "I did not choose this story" or "Do not hold me responsible or accountable for it." This kind of disclaimer implies that the tale was almost foisted upon the narrator as if she would rather tell a more affirming narrative.

Both these early short stories are allegories of ancient folktales of the Arawak Indians and the Europeans, rewritten as twentieth- or twenty-first-century parables. However, most of Brodber's short stories in *The World Is a High Hill* are, like those of her sister, realistic tales of community life, particularly of rural women in Jamaica.

"Rosa," from *The World Is a High Hill*, incorporates many of the ideas that Brodber develops in more detail in her novels. The idea of the transmigration of souls that she discusses extensively in *Louisiana* is an important part of the story. As Brodber told the critic Carolyn Cooper in an interview, "Rosa" is a story she started writing on the back of a questionnaire she used as a community social worker; when she sent the story to the International Festival in 1972, she was surprised when it was accepted.[47] Brodber includes in the story several characters from St. Mary Parish with its history of slavery and its diverse population. Zackie, Rosa's isolated neighbor, belongs to one of the oldest families of Greenville Town of Epsom in St. Mary. His grandfather was the Greenville resident who had first settled in the village when enslaved persons were freed.

Zackie's grandfather, a former slave driver, no longer had any reason to live in the area, so he decided to start sugar production on the property. Because Zackie's family had been a founding family, he possessed a sense of superiority, even though he was actually quite poor. However, Zackie stuck to sugarcane production even when the crop started to bring little money, not nearly as much as bananas. Most of his cousins had gone into harvesting bananas because of the success of the United Fruit Company. Zackie, though, does not have any motivation to change; he continues to live in his stone-nog house on his very poor ground and cannot keep up with his more prosperous cousins.

The much poorer woman, Rosa, dreams one night that she should go over to Zackie's house and help him make something of himself and his property. Surprisingly, after she fixes up the house and reorganizes the farm area so that Zackie begins to grow yams and bananas, as well as sugar, and he starts to bring in much more money, they marry. The story becomes like an ancient Confucian tale that teaches values of generosity, truth, and honor, with the impoverished Rosa as instructor. Zackie realizes that he has found a good wife who saved his life and made him know that "God is good. All the time."

Another of the stories in *The World Is a High Hill*, "Kishwana," addresses the subject of what Carolyn Cooper calls "border crossing."[48] The characters Kishwana and Arthur come from two dramatically different levels of society, yet they end up climbing the hill between them and meeting each other along the way. The story is very much like many of Pollard's stories in *Considering Woman*. The well-to-do Arthur in "Kishwana" feels determined to know the poor community that Kishwana is from, the type of rural life where there are no inside toilets and no running water. Because Kishwana is intelligent and creative in all ways, she manages her studies along with helping to raise her little siblings and taking care of the chores that her mother and their one-room house demand. She does not feel ashamed of her standard of living, even though Arthur is the son of a middle-class mother and father. His mother persuades her friend Belfoot, candidate for a current community election, to help Kishwana gain admission into one of the good high schools in Kingston. The reader discovers that the politician is really Kishwana's biological father, and finally, he and Kishwana's mother marry. Kishwana ends up marrying Arthur and still takes care of her brothers and sisters as well. Again, the poor woman is a hero.

The story "Kishwana" closely follows a linear narrative in what is a romance of several rural inhabitants, but it has an ending that is more hopeful than typical. It is not at all the kind of allegorical and mythical tale that Brodber wrote in her early short fiction, such as "One Bubby Susan" and "Sleeping's Beauty." Most of Brodber's stories in *The World Is a High Hill* are similar in many ways. As Jamaican historian Verena Shepherd says in the foreword:

> The world is indeed a high hill—to climb—especially for "low bud-get people" in Buju Bannon's creative formulation [twenty-first-century Jamaican musician]: black, rural, slavery-descended, mis-educated, under-educated, and downright, working-class people: men and women. Featured in these stories completed the steep incline because they had no choice. They know that for upward social mobility, migration should take place. They also demonstrated by their lives that migration . . . had to be on their own terms.[49]

Indeed, migration can come in the form of moving to another nation or to another part of the Caribbean.

CONCLUSIONS

The sisters Erna Brodber and Velma Pollard have created narratives and poetry that develop ideas of culture and folklore in rural Jamaica. They center on their home village of Woodside in St. Mary Parish but move the settings of the fiction to other regions of Jamaica and other Caribbean islands, as well as metropolises in the United States, Canada, and the United Kingdom. Yet, there is always in the background a sense that West African culture, religion, and folklore pervade their lives. Much of Jamaican culture, particularly in the rural areas, is based on African beliefs and folk culture.

I first became interested in this subject when I married a Jamaican man. I did not know much about Jamaica as I was born and grew up in Florence, South Carolina. My husband and I were fascinated by each other's cultures. In addition to this, we met in Massachusetts, where we both went to college, and then came to live in New Orleans, Louisiana, where my Jamaican in-laws lived. Because of this exciting amalgamation of places and cultures, I grew interested in studying place and culture, particularly in literature, my major in college and graduate school. My husband had a fascination with history and American studies also.

With all this in mind, it is easy to understand that my first book was a study of place and culture. It was called *The Myth of New Orleans: A Study of Place in Fiction.* I continued to write articles about culture and place in the literature of African American writers, mostly women. But when I attended a conference on Black women writers in Flint, Michigan, in 1984, I heard a paper on Erna Brodber's first novel, *Jane and Louisa Will Soon Come Home.* I thought the language and the waves of thought were beautiful and decided to learn more about this writer.

When I returned home to New Orleans, I told my husband and in-laws about the novel, and they said that they knew the writer: she was my husband's second cousin, a relative of my father-in-law's mother, a Brodber. She has a sister, Velma Pollard, who is also a writer. I met Pollard first at Caribbean Studies Association Conferences in St. Kitts and Belize and, more recently, at a Furious Flower Conference in Maryland. I began to read Pollard's poetry and then moved to her short stories and novels. I set about reading all the novels of Erna Brodber, but I soon found that the sisters never stop writing. In addition to their fiction and poetry, there is much nonfiction to read.

The sisters' fiction and poetry teach much about spirit—spirit theft and spirit possession, and spirits existing through time from Africa to the present. Brodber's narratives also show the communication of the living and the dead, as expressed in most of her works, from *Jane and Louisa* to *Louisiana* and *Nothing's Mat.* Pollard also shows an interest in spirit in her poetry, fiction, and nonfiction, but in a more traditional sense. She apparently favors the Anglican faith, as is clear in her novel *Homestretch*, as the protagonists who return home to the Jamaican rural area attend an Anglican church and participate with fervor. She also expresses in her poetry a love of nature in Jamaica and other Caribbean nations. She said in an interview that she finds writing itself to be therapeutic.[50]

Brodber's and Pollard's protagonists and settings are based on people from the African diaspora, that is, communities from west, central, and south Africa who came to the Americas via the Atlantic slave trade or as indentured servants. Pollard also writes about the new African Jamaican diaspora, the descendants of those of the early diaspora who migrated to other nations but returned to Jamaica, at least for certain periods, expressing the commonality of the African diaspora culture and the African diaspora of the United States.

The culture of the African diaspora values family, knowledge beyond the senses, telling stories and parables, wittiness, and trickiness, with a respect for myth and history. Anancy, the Akan folklore character, is also important to Jamaican culture. The spider is associated with wisdom, storytelling, and trickiness. Both Pollard and Brodber employ Anancy and his tales in their fiction and poetry, or they point out the Anancy nature of certain characters, such as Baba in Brodber's *Jane and Louisa* or the fly in Pollard's poem by that name. The authors value the folklore character's trickiness and wisdom, and the characters of their stories often tell fantastic tales, such as a woman having a callaloo plant-child because she ate too much callaloo or a chicken flying so high that she cured a woman's illness.

Both Pollard and Brodber describe the lives of women of the African diaspora in their fiction and poetry. They point out that women must be firm in their sense of self and place in the family and society and save themselves from smothering in the patriarchal society of Jamaica. Many women characters in Pollard's short stories and poetry must break out of the cage of marriage, as she describes in her stories in "The Cage" section of her first collection of stories, *Considering Woman*. Brodber speaks of the patriarchal demands of the community in her stories "One Bubby Susan" and "Kishwana." Repeatedly, they emphasize that women must speak out to be heard.

Pollard has a fascination with language and sound in her works and those of her sister. She also has recognized the importance of sound and music as a connection between Caribbean and African American literature. In her article "The American in Anglophone Caribbean Women Writers: Bridges of Sound," Pollard discusses Paule Marshall's *Praisesong for the Widow* and her sister Erna's *Louisiana*.[51] In the article, Pollard explores a sonic connection between Caribbean and African American writers due to their African origins. In Pollard's works such as *Dread Talk*, she amplifies the echoes between Dub

Poetry of the Caribbean and rap and hip-hop music of the United States. She accentuates the relation of sound in her own poetry to that of the United States and Africa.[52]

Throughout their fiction and poetry, the sisters convey much interest in Black nationalist Marcus Garvey, who is a Jamaican hero. Garvey is an illustrious symbol of Black liberation. The sisters are also enamored of the idea of trickiness and rebellion, as seen in the stories of Anancy, the Ghanaian and Jamaican spirit of cleverness. Pollard went so far as to publish a collection of Anancy stories, which she entitled *Anansesem*.[53] Both writers draw upon tales of Anancy throughout their fiction and poetry.

Throughout their work, both writers also show a fascination with historical resistance, such as the recurrent interest in the Morant Bay Rebellion, which took place in St. Thomas Parish in 1865. The event involved the rebellion of newly freed Africans and Afro-Jamaicans when the colonial powers attempted to impose their power over the free people of Jamaica. The historical opposition of freedom and powerful elites has been manifested in many rebellions, strikes, and other protests, such as the demonstrations around the Caribbean after the assassination of Walter Rodney in 1980.[54] This profuse history of Black resistance has deeply affected Brodber and Pollard.

Although both writers pay attention to male heroes and even figures from history and folklore in their writings, the protagonists and the main points of view in most of their fiction and poetry are women. In Brodber's novels, the protagonists even bear similar names, such as Nellie and Ella, although, in the later novels, they are named Queenie and Princess. Throughout their short fiction, the sisters stress the problems of rural Jamaican women, particularly the restrictions, social and economic, in a patriarchal society. Several of Pollard's stories portray the oppression of Jamaican women; examples are "My Mother (for Marjorie)" and "Gran." Yet, there is a certain resilience. In Brodber's stories "Rosa" and "Kishwana," poor women emerge as heroic protagonists. Both Pollard and Brodber write about coming out of "the *kumbla*" and finding their identity.[55] They must fight against a patriarchal society and establish their individuality but also their place in the community and the family, both present and the past. In one poem, Pollard's speaker realizes that Jamaica is not just tall, "it is tallawah."

The sisters celebrating. Private Collection of Velma Pollard. Courtesy of the Pollard Family.

The influence of African folklore and culture and that of the sister-writers' home in Woodside, St. Mary, Jamaica on their writing is important. The sisters' projections of their homeland and their writing themes and narrative strategies have influenced educators, scholars, and writers. The African nation of Kenya has mandated Pollard's novel *Homestretch* as a required novel for its secondary schools. Pollard has also been recognized for her poetry and its cross-fertilization at the two Furious Flower conferences, originally organized by the literary scholar Joanne Gabbin.[56] At the 2014 conference, Pollard received a Lifetime Achievement Award and appeared on the panel "Cross-Pollination in the Diaspora" about the different nationalities and ideologies that contribute to the strength of Black poetry of the diaspora.

Brodber has also been the subject of much scholarly inquiry. Moreover, she remains influential to many writers of the next generation. One of these writers is Marlon James, whose novel *A Brief History of Seven Killings* won the 2015 Man Booker Prize and the OCM Bocas Prize for Caribbean Literature. Recently, James named Brodber's *Myal* one of "Five Jamaican Novels You Should Read" because of her unique and early use of speculative fiction.[57] According to the American-born Canadian writer and editor Jia Tolentino, "There is a long counter-tradition of speculative fiction by black writers," which extends from W. E. B. Du Bois's 1920 apocalypse story "The Comet" through such major figures of the genre as Samuel Delany and Octavia Butler.[58] Many writers of the twenty-first century have recognized the influence of Brodber in this tradition of speculative fiction.

This book is the first to examine Velma Pollard's writing on a par with that of her sister, Erna Brodber. Along with spirits, there is Brodber's interest in temporal progression and time shifts, so that characters often live in the present, the past, and future.

NOTES

CHAPTER 1. WOODSIDE: THE LIVED AND IMAGINED HOMELAND IN
THE FICTION AND POETRY OF ERNA BRODBER AND VELMA POLLARD

1. Authors who have studied Brodber's work with spirits include the following:
Melvin B. Rahming, "Towards a Critical Theory of Spirit: The Insistent Demands
of Erna Brodber's *Myal*," in *Changing Currents: Caribbean Literary and Cultural
Criticism*, ed. Emily Williams and Melvin Rahming (Ewing, NJ: Africa World
Press, 2006); Neil Ten Kortenaar, "Foreign Possessions: Erna Brodber's *Myal*—the
Medium and the Message," *Ariel* 30, no. 4 (October 1990): 51–74; Helen Tiffin,
"Cold Hearts and Foreign Tongues: Recitation and Reclamation of the Female
Body in the Works of Erna Brodber and Jamaica Kincaid," *Callaloo* 6, no. 4: 909–
21; and Anne Margaret Castro, "Sounding Out Spirit Thievery in Erna Brodber's
Myal," *Journal of West Indian Literature* 23, no. 1–2 (April–November 2015): 106–20.

2. Brodber, *Jane and Louisa Will Soon Come Home* (London: New Beacon
Books, 1980) and *Nothing's Mat* (Kingston, Jamaica: University of the West Indies
Press, 2014).

3. Pollard, *Homestretch* (London: Longman Group, 1994).

4. Brodber, "Fiction in the Scientific Procedure," in *Caribbean Women Writers:
Essays from the First International Conference*, ed. Selwyn R. Cudjoe (Wellesley,
MA: Callalouxx Publications, 1990), 166.

5. Allison Donnell, "What It Means to Stay: Reterritorializing the Black
Atlantic in Erna Brodber's Writing of the Local," *Third World Quarterly* 26, no. 3
(2005): 479–86.

6. June E. Roberts, *Reading Erna Brodber: Uniting the Black Diaspora through
Folk Culture and Religion* (Westport, CT: Praeger, 2006), 91–100.

7. Brodber, "Writing Your Village History," in *The Continent of Black
Consciousness* (London: New Beacon Books, 2003), 160–79.

8. Brodber, *Woodside, Pear Tree Grove P.O.* (Kingston, Jamaica: University of
the West Indies Press, 2004), 104–22.

9. Brodber, *Woodside*, vi.

10. Brodber, *Woodside*, vii.

11. Violet Harrington Bryan, interview with the authors, July 2005.

12. Evelyn O'Callaghan, "Erna Brodber," in *Fifty Caribbean Writers: A Bio-Bibliographical Critical Sourcebook*, ed. Daryl Cumber Dance (Westport, CT: Greenwood Press, 1986), 71–82.

13. Daryl Cumber Dance, "Conversation with Pam Mordecai and Velma Pollard," in *New World Adams* (London: Peepal Tree Press, 1992), 182–95.

14. Peter Manuel, *Caribbean Currents: Caribbean Music from Rumba to Reggae* (Philadelphia: Temple University Press, 2006), 192.

15. Brodber, "Fiction in the Scientific Procedure," 166.

16. Brodber, "Fiction in the Scientific Procedure," 166.

17. Pollard, *Karl*, Edicion Bilingue (Havana, Cuba: Casa da las Americas, 1992); Pollard, *Karl and Other Stories* (London: Longman Caribbean Writers, 1994); Pollard, *Homestretch*.

18. Dance, "Conversation," 188.

19. Dance, "Conversation," 188.

20. Dance, "Conversation," 186.

21. Dance, "Conversation," 186–95.

22. Stuart Hall, "Cultural Identity and Diaspora," in *The Postcolonial Studies Reader*, ed. Bill Ashcroft, Gareth Griffin, and Helen Tiffin, 2nd ed. (New York: Routledge, 1995), 438.

23. Brodber, "Writing Your Village History."

24. Brodber, "Writing Your Village History," 163.

25. Brodber, *Woodside*, 20–23.

26. Brodber, *The Second Generation of Freemen in Jamaica, 1907–1944* (Gainesville: University Press of Florida, 2004), 1–20.

27. Annie Neugebauer, "What Is Speculative Fiction?" (blog), March 24, 2014, anniebauer.com/2014/03/24/what-is-speculative-fiction?

28. Marie Sairsingh, "Diasporic Connections: Erna Brodber and Toni Morrison's Literary Explorations of Black Existentiality," *CLA Journal* 56, no. 4 (June 2013): 315–28.

29. Brodber, *Woodside*, 51.

30. Brodber, *Woodside*, 113.

31. Interview with the author, 2005.

32. Brodber, *Woodside*, vii.

33. Keshia Abraham, "Interview with Erna Brodber," *BOMB: Artists in Conversation* (Winter 2004).

34. Quoted in Catherine John, "Caribbean Organic Intellectual: The Legacy and Challenge of Erna Brodber's Life Work," *Small Axe: A Caribbean Journal of Criticism* 38 (November 2012).

35. Violet Harrington Bryan, "'Tomorrow's Spaces' in the Poetry of Jamaican Writer Velma Pollard," *Xavier Review* 33, no. 1 (Spring 2013): 69–77.

36. Pollard, "Our Mother," in *Crown Point and Other Poems* (London: Peepal Press, 1988), 79.

CHAPTER 2. VELMA POLLARD'S *KARL* AND ERNA BRODBER'S *JANE AND LOUISA WILL SOON COME HOME*

1. Adlith Brown, "Economic Policy and the IMF and Jamaica," *Regional Monetary Studies* 30, no. 4 (December 1981): 1–51.

2. Brian Meeks, "Michael Manley's Vision," *Jacobin*, May 17, 2017, https://jacobinmag.com/2017/05/michael-manley-jamaica-non-aligned-movement-imf-austerity-imperialism.

3. Barry Chevannes, *Rastafari: Roots and Ideology* (Syracuse, NY: Syracuse University Press, 1994); and Leonard E. Barrett, *The Rastafarians: Twentieth Anniversary Edition* (Boston: Beacon Press, 1997). The Rastafarians were especially popular in Jamaica in the 1970s, with the election of Michael Manley as prime minister in 1972 and the popularity of reggae music by Bob Marley and others.

4. The seven National Jamaican Heroes are Marcus Garvey, Sir Alexander Bustamante, Norman Washington Marley, Samuel Sharpe, Paul Bogle, George William Gordon, and Nanny of the Maroons. http://aglobalworld.com/holidays-around-the-world/jamaica-national-heroes-day/.

5. See Anita M. Waters, *Race, Class, and Political Symbols: Rastafari and Reggae in Jamaican Politics* (New Brunswick, NJ: Transaction Publishers, 1985) for a discussion of how politicians used the ideas of Rastafarianism and reggae.

6. References to this novella will be to this edition: Pollard, *Karl*, rev. ed. (London: Mango Publishing, 2001).

7. A bildungsroman is the story of a child growing up or gaining his or her maturity.

8. According to a July 17, 2013, article in the *Jamaica Gleaner*: "When the Panama Canal was under construction by the United States between 1904 and its opening in 1914, many Jamaican laborers worked on this project in one of Jamaican early waves of migration."

9. Jared McAllister, "Caribbeat: Mr. President, Black Caribbean workers 'dug out' the Panama Canal for America," *New York Daily News*, July 5, 2020.

10. Pollard, *Karl*, 28.

11. Being made a pupil-teacher was a way that a teacher postponed a bright student's graduation from a free school because of a lack of money. When the

student won the award of becoming a pupil-teacher, the student was normally able to later win a scholarship to a university, perhaps in a foreign country. The concept is mentioned in many Caribbean novels. It is significant in Erna Brodber's novel *Myal* when the teacher Holness was able to keep Anita in school until she won a scholarship to do further study.

12. Pollard, *Karl*, 31.

13. Peter Manuel, *Caribbean Currents: Caribbean Music from Rumba to Reggae* (Philadelphia: Temple University Press, 2006), 191–99.

14. Erna Brodber, *Woodside, Pear Tree Grove P.O.* (Kingston, Jamaica: University of the West Indies Press, 2004), 31.

15. Pollard, *Karl*, 46.

16. Pollard, *Karl*, 42.

17. Pollard, *Karl*, 54.

18. Pollard, *Karl*, 54.

19. Pollard, *Karl*, 45.

20. Pollard, *Karl*, title page.

21. Pollard, *Karl*, 4.

22. Pollard, *Dread Talk: The Language of the Rastafari* (Kingston, Jamaica: Canoe Press, 2004), 4.

23. Pollard, *Dread Talk*, 18.

24. Eric Doumerc, "Rastafarians in Post-Independence Caribbean Poetry in English (the 1960s and the 1970s) from Pariahs to Cultural Creators," *Miranda Revues Org*, April 2011.

25. Pollard, *Dread Talk*, 73. Mervyn Morris published several books of poetry and received a Jamaican Order of Merit for his work. See https://poetryarchive .org/poet/mervyn-morris.

26. Pollard, *Karl*, 11.

27. Chevannes, *Rastafari*, 208. Chevannes writes: "In theory, all non-Rastafari are a part of 'Babylon,' a part of the oppressive order, and are therefore on a personal level likely to be subject to verbal and other nonviolent forms of aggression such as the tense facial expression commonly referred to as 'screwface.'"

28. Pollard, *Karl*, 45.

29. Pollard, *Karl*, 42.

30. Pollard, *Karl*, 5.

31. Pollard, *Karl*, 4–5.

32. Pollard, *Karl*, 72.

33. Pollard, *Karl*, 73.

34. Pollard, *Karl*, 75.

35. Jamaican Anglican hymnals began to include reggae songs in the late twentieth century. See "Jamaica's Anglican church to modernize hymnals with

reggae songs," *Religion News Blog*, August 6, 2007, https://www.religionnewsblog .com/18943/reggae-hymns.

36. Holger Henke, *Between Self-Determination and Dependency: Jamaica's Foreign Relations, 1972–1989* (Kingston, Jamaica: University of the West Indies Press, 2000).

37. Brodber, *Jane and Louisa Will Soon Come Home* (London: New Beacon Books, 1980), 123. Citations to this novel are from this edition.

38. Brodber, *Jane and Louisa*, 123.

39. Brodber, *Jane and Louisa*, 9.

40. Brodber, *Jane and Louisa*, 8.

41. Rhonda Cobham, "Revisioning Our Kumblas: Transforming Feminist and Nationalist Agendas in Three Caribbean Women's Texts," *Callaloo* 16, no. 1 (Winter 1993): 49.

42. Brodber, *Jane and Louisa*, 143.

43. Brodber, *Jane and Louisa*, 16–17.

44. Brodber, *Jane and Louisa*, 14.

45. Brodber, *Jane and Louisa*, 14. On obeah, see Diana Paton, *The Cultural Politics of Obeah: Religion, Colonialism, and Modernity in the Caribbean World* (New York: Cambridge University Press, 2015). The obeah practitioner could practice through spells and sacrifices. The death of Lester, a young man who disappeared after a short trip, would remain a mystery for generations.

46. Brodber, *Jane and Louisa*, 26.

47. Brodber, *Jane and Louisa*, 14.

48. Kevin Arthur Cryderman, "The Language of *Jane and Louisa*," 2000, www .postcolonialweb.org/caribbean/brodber/kcry2.html.

49. The thinkers were colleagues and friends of Erna Brodber during Jamaica's post-independence. They proceeded to teach in universities in the Caribbean and the US. See Henry Paget, "Economic Nationalism and Socialism: A Tribute to Norman Girvan," *The CLR James Journal* 20, no. 1–2 (Fall 2014): 49–58.

50. June E. Roberts, *Reading Erna Brodber: Uniting the Black Diaspora through Folk Culture and Religion* (Westport, CT: Praeger, 2006). According to Roberts, the period between the 1960s and the early 1970s "was marked by the intervention of national independence and black power, Rastafarianism and reggae" (13).

51. Brodber, *Jane and Louisa*, 134–35.

52. Daria Zheltukhina, "Rhythmicity and Broken Narrative as a Means of Portraying Identity Crisis in Erna Brodber's *Jane and Louisa Will Soon Come Home*," in *Culture and Religion* (Westport, CT: Praeger, 2006), xiii; Evelyn O'Callaghan, "Erna Brodber," in *Fifty Caribbean Writers*, ed. Daryl Cumber Dance (Westport, CT: Greenwood Press, 1986).

53. Quoted in Petal Samuel, "'Put Your Bucket Down': A Conversation with Erna Brodber," *SX Salon*, June 2015, http://smallaxe.net/sxsalon/interviews/put -your-bucket-down.

54. Roberts, *Reading Erna Brodber*, 120.

55. Brodber, *Jane and Louisa*, 52.

56. Roberts, *Reading Erna Brodber*, 120.

57. Daryl Cumber Dance, "Who Was Cock Robin? A New Reading of Erna Brodber's *Jane and Louisa Will Soon Come Home*," *CLA Journal* 50, no. 1 (September 2006): 20–36.

58. Brodber, *Jane and Louisa*, 62.

59. Brodber, *Jane and Louisa*, 60.

60. See Velma Pollard, *Anansesem: A Collection of Caribbean Folk Tales, Legends, and Poems for Juniors* (Kingston, Jamaica: Longman Jamaica, 1985). Anancy is the trickster spider spirit originally conceived by the Ashanti in Ghana. For more information, see https://jamaicans.com/?s=Anancy.

61. Brodber, *Jane and Louisa*, 76.

62. Brodber, *Jane and Louisa*, 134.

63. Brodber, *Jane and Louisa*, 135.

64. The end of slavery in the Caribbean took place in 1838, although a compromise situation, with the freed people serving as paid apprentices began in 1834. Brodber writes about the situation of freedom and Black people finding their way in her 2007 novel, *The Rainmaker's Mistake*.

65. The Morant Bay Rebellion occurred in 1865 and is referenced in many of Brodber's and Pollard's works.

66. Roberts, *Reading Erna Brodber*, 91–100.

67. Brodber, *Jane and Louisa*, 138.

68. Brodber, *Jane and Louisa*, 139.

69. Brodber, *Jane and Louisa*, 78.

70. Brodber, *Jane and Louisa*, 81.

71. The ancestors appear to Nellie as pictures from "the moving camera."

72. Brodber, *Jane and Louisa*, 81.

73. Brodber, *Jane and Louisa*, 133.

74. Brodber, *Jane and Louisa*, 133.

75. Brodber, *Jane and Louisa*, 133.

76. Brodber, *Jane and Louisa*, 147.

77. Brodber, *Jane and Louisa*, 147.

CHAPTER 3. SPIRIT THEFT AND SPIRIT POSSESSION IN ERNA
BRODBER'S *MYAL* AND *LOUISIANA*

1. Anne Margaret Castro, "Sounding Out Spirit Thievery in Erna Brodber's *Myal*," *Journal of West Indian Literature* 23, no. 1–2 (April–November 2015): 106–20.

2. Brodber, *Myal* (London: New Beacon Books, 1988), 8; Pollard, *Dread Talk: The Language of the Rastafari* (Kingston, Jamaica: Canoe Press, 1994). Citations to these works are to these editions.

3. See Margarite Fernandez-Omos and Lizabeth Paravisini-Gerbert, ed., *Healing Cultures: Art and Religion as Curative Practices in the Caribbean and Its Diaspora* (New York: Palgrave Press, 2001).

4. Margarite Fernandez-Omos and Lizabeth Paravisini-Gerbert, *Creole Religions in the Caribbean: An Introduction from Vodou and Santeria to Obeah and Santeria* (New York: New York University Press, 2003).

5. Brodber, *Myal*, 3.

6. See Neil Ten Kortenaar, "Foreign Possessions: Erna Brodber's 'Myal,' the Medium, and the Message," *Ariel: A Review of International English Literature* 30, no. 4 (October 1999): 53.

7. Marwan M. Kraidy, "Communication," *Theory* 12, no. 3 (August 2002): 316–39.

8. Brodber, *Myal*, 1. "These people" refers to the biracial nature of Ella O'Brien. This example of hybridity is evident in the mixed cultures that populate this area of Jamaica. Mass Cyrus's phrase refers also to the hybridity of the Jamaican culture, particularly in the rural areas.

9. Brodber, *Myal*, 2.

10. The word "etheric" here symbolizes the energy of the Myalist ritual, and Brodber is also referring to the hybridity or diversity of the Jamaican culture, particularly in the rural areas.

11. Kipling's poem was written in 1899 to celebrate Queen Victoria's reign. She was queen when slavery was abolished in Great Britain in all its colonies in 1838. Queen Victoria is also referenced in *Jane and Louisa* and many of Brodber's other books. Kipling later modified his poem to reflect the American takeover of the Philippines. "The white man's burden" became a synonym for imperialism. The young Ella did not realize that she was in fact describing herself in the unfavorable light of being "the white man's burden" and siding with the colonial powers that were running and ruining her life and still getting the credit for taking on the heavy burden of caring for the darker people, the "other."

12. The term "white Jamaican" is a frequently used term in Jamaican Creole language, but its meaning is disputed.

13. Brodber, *Myal*, 23.

14. Homi Bhabha, *The Location of Culture* (New York: Routledge, 2004), 53–56.

15. "Linguistic ritual" is the game that Maydene Brassington and Amy Holness are playing with language in these pages of *Myal*. See Catherine A. John, *Clear Word and Third Sight: Folk Groundins and Diasporic Consciousness in African Caribbean Writing* (Durham, NC: Duke University Press, 2003).

16. Brodber, *Myal*, 26–27.

17. Brodber, *Myal*, 7.

18. Anancy (also spelled Ananse or Anansi) is a character in Caribbean and African folklore, a cunning trickster generally depicted as a spider, though he often transforms into human form. The subject of many Anancy stories, the character has its origins among the Ashanti of West Africa. See Molefi Kete Asante, "Ananse: Folklore Character," Britannica.com, accessed April 8, 2021, https://www.britannica.com/topic/Ananse.

19. Brodber, *Myal*, 79–80.

20. Brodber, *Myal*, 84.

21. Brodber, *Myal*, 12.

22. For more information on pupil-teachers in Jamaica schools, see the discussion of Velma Pollard's novella *Karl* in Chapter 2, note 11.

23. Brodber, *Myal*, 30.

24. Brodber, *Myal*, 30.

25. Brodber, *Myal*, 28.

26. Brodber, *Myal*, 30.

27. Brodber, *Myal*, 32.

28. Brodber, *Myal*, 36. Reverend Simpson's words as he wrote his Sunday sermon on "Let my people go" refers to "that St. Ann. Fellow that start up this Aboukir Institute, to Marcus Garvey, who was born in St. Ann's Bay, Jamaica, in 1887." Garvey was a leader of Pan-Africanism and founder of the Universal Negro Improvement Association (UNIA) and believed that African Americans should return to their homeland in Africa and increase their strength as a people. Both Garvey and the UNIA are of major importance in several of Brodber's novels.

29. Stealing the Africans' stools is associated with the Europeans' stealing the chiefs' stools in Ghana and other African countries, but also references the stealing of the Golden Stool of the Ashanti, which became an African legend, and the tradition of Europeans' stealing the natural resources of Africans.

30. The first slave ships from Africa arrived in Jamaica in 1672 when the Royal African Company delivered captive Africans to both Barbados and Jamaica. See Brendan Wolfe, "Slave Ships and the Middle Passage," in *Encyclopedia Virginia* (Charlottesville: Virginia Foundation for the Humanities, 2013).

31. Bill Evans, "Tacky's Slave Rebellion," Jamaicans.com, accessed April 8, 2021, https://jamaicans.com/tackys_rebellion/.

32. Brodber, *Myal*, 4.

33. The Witch, sometimes called the Medium, of Endor was a woman who called up the ghost of the recently deceased Samuel at the demand of King Saul of the Kingdom of Israel. See 1 Samuel 25:28–30.

34. The idea that there are more ways of knowing than are accessible to the five senses is an essential theme of Brodber's writing.

35. Brodber, *Myal*, 94–95.

36. See Ten Kortenaar, "Foreign Possessions," 53.

37. Brodber, *Myal*, 58–59.

38. The old man, Mass Levi, is using the ritual of obeah to rape Anita and access her power as a young woman full of vitality.

39. Brodber, *Myal*, 65.

40. Brodber, *Myal*, 67.

41. Rahming, "Towards a Critical Theory of Spirit: The Insistent Demands of Erna Brodber's *Myal*," in *Changing Currents: Caribbean Literary and Cultural Criticism*, ed. Emily Williams and Melvin Rahmind (Ewing, NJ: Africa World Press, 2006).

42. "The influences that shaped Kumina landed in the 1850s with the arrival of African indentured immigrants from the Congo region of Central Africa during the immediate postemancipation period. Kumina took root in St. Thomas where a number of the immigrants settled." "Kumina in Jamaica," accessed April 8, 2021, digjamaica.com/m/indigenous-religions-in-jamaica/kumina.

43. Brodber, *Myal*, 72.

44. Brodber, *Myal*, 73.

45. Brodber, *Myal*, 73.

46. Brodber, *Myal*, 77.

47. Brodber, *Myal*, 78.

48. June E. Roberts, *Reading Erna Brodber: Uniting the Black Diaspora through Folk Culture and Religion* (Westport, CT: Praeger, 2006), 111.

49. Roberts, *Reading Erna Brodber*, 111.

50. Brodber, *Myal*, 96.

51. Brodber, *Myal*, 111. Whitehall refers to a government building where many important governmental issues were discussed, including education on the island.

52. Citations to this novel are to this edition: Brodber, *Louisiana* (Jackson: University Press of Mississippi, 1997). The adjective "mystical" as I use it here suggests mysteriousness associated with an occult, or African-derived, religion.

53. Brodber, *Woodside, Pear Tree Grove P.O.* (Kingston, Jamaica: University of the West Indies Press, 2004), 49.

54. Brodber, "Fiction in the Scientific Procedure," in *Caribbean Women Writers*, ed. Selwyn R. Cudjoe (Wellesley, MA: Callalouxx Publications, 1990), 164–68. In this essay, Brodber called herself an "intellectual worker" and anthropologist who wrote fiction to provide sociological cases for her students. See also Samantha Pinto, *Difficult Diasporas: The Transnational Feminist Aesthetic* (New York: New York University Press, 2013).

55. Brodber, *Louisiana*, 18.

56. Brodber, *Louisiana*, 12.

57. Brodber, *Louisiana*, 22.

58. Brodber, *Louisiana*, 31.

59. Brodber, *Louisiana*, 45–46.

60. Osbey, "Invocation," *All Saints: New and Selected Poems* (Baton Rouge: Louisiana State University Press, 1985), 1.

61. Madame Marie is probably based on the historical Marie Laveau, the legendary priestess of American voodoo, who lived in Congo Square in the Treme district of New Orleans in the nineteenth century. Marie Laveau was actually two women with the same name: a mother and her daughter, both Creoles. See Martha Ward, *Voodoo Queen: The Spirited Lives of Marie Laveau* (Jackson: University Press of Mississippi, 2004).

62. For "Sammy Dead" lyrics, see "Desmond Dekker and the Specials," a popular Jamaica folk song often sung during funerals and sometime sung in mento in the second half of the twentieth century. The lyrics are in part: "Sammy plant piece a corn dung a gully mm. / An I bear till I kill poor Sammy mm mm. / Sammy dead, Sammy dead. Sammy dead oh, mm.mm."

63. See Jeremie Kroubo Dagnini, "Traditional Folklore and the Question of History in Erna Brodber's *Louisiana*," *Journal of Pan-African Studies* 4, no. 8 (December 2011): 34.

64. Nilofar Akhtar, "Stephen Gill's *Immigrant*: A Study in Diasporic Consciousness," accessed April 8, 2021, https://stephengill.ca/2008-winter/Nilofar%20Akhtar %20.htm.

65. The headquarters of the United Fruit Company was in New Orleans. See Steven Palmer and Iván Molina, eds., *The Costa Rica Reader: History, Culture, Politics* (Durham, NC: Duke University Press, 2009).

66. Brodber, *Louisiana*, 83.

67. Brodber, *Louisiana*, 88.

68. Brodber, *Louisiana*, 104.

69. Brodber, *Louisiana*, 104.

70. Brodber was teaching her sociology students the way to work with "dissociated children" when she decided to present her ideas in the novel *Jane and Louisa Will Soon Come Home* instead of in an academic study.

71. *Wiktionary* (accessed January 26, 2017) defines "samfie man" as "a confidence trickster, especially one who pretends to have supernatural powers."

72. See Simboonath Singh, "Resistance, Essentialism, and Empowerment in Black Nationalist Discourse in the African Diaspora," *Journal of African American Studies* 8, no. 3 (Winter 2004): 30.

73. Roberts, *Reading Erna Brodber*, 216.

74. Brodber, *Louisiana*, 80.

75. Brodber, *Louisiana*, 81.

76. Brodber, *Louisiana*, 82.

77. Brodber, *Louisiana*, 99–100.

78. See John DeSantis, *The Thibodaux Massacre* (Columbia, SC: History Press Library Editions, 2016). The Thibodaux Massacre of sugarcane workers who went

on a three-week strike in LaFourche, Terrebonne, St. Mary, and Iberia parishes in Louisiana took place on or about November 22, 1887. Over three hundred African American workers were killed.

79. Brodber, *Louisiana*, 3–4.

CHAPTER 4. MIGRATION, RETURN, AND "TOMORROW'S SPACES" IN VELMA POLLARD'S WRITINGS

1. See Chapter 1 for an overview of Pollard's many works.

2. Stuart Hall, "Cultural Identity and Diaspora," in *The Post-Colonial Studies Reader*, ed. Bill Ashcroft, Garreth Griffiths, and Helen Tiffin, 2nd ed. (New York: Routledge, 1995), 438.

3. Brent Hayes Edwards, *The Practice of Diaspora* (Cambridge, MA: Harvard University Press, 2003).

4. Leith Dunn and Suzanne Scafe, "African-Caribbean Women: Migration, Diaspora, Post-Diaspora," *Caribbean Review of Gender Studies* 13: 1–16.

5. Citations to this novel are to this edition: Pollard, *Homestretch* (London: Longman Group, 1994).

6. *Homestretch* is currently one of the optional literature set books for secondary school students in Kenya in Africa.

7. Mike Phillips with Trevor Phillips, *Windrush: The Irresistible Rise of Multi-Racial Britain* (London: HarperCollins, 1998).

8. Brodber, *Jane and Louisa Will Soon Come Home* (London: New Beacon Books, 1980). Galliwasps are reptiles that are the subject of folklore; see Darren Nash, "The Galliwasps," *Scientific American Blog Network*, September 9, 2015.

9. The epigraph suggests the couple's joy at returning to their home and stepping again on their native soil. Their hearts beat like a metronome because of living the dream that has been a part of their lives for all those thirty years away in England.

10. David Cowan, "The Heart's Metronome: Dennis Scott and Jamaican Lyrics," in *The Prospect of Lyric* (Dallas: Dallas Institute Publications), 371.

11. Pollard, *Homestretch*, 13.

12. Pollard, *Homestretch*, 5.

13. Pollard, *Homestretch*, 44.

14. Pollard, *Homestretch*, 20.

15. Heritage Week in Jamaica is a week-long festivity to celebrate events and significant groups of Jamaican history. See https://www.my-island-jamaica.com /what-is-heritage-day-in-jamaica.html#.

16. Pollard, *Homestretch*, 122. Compare Edith's comment about "the half" to the phrase "the half that's never been told" used repeatedly by Ole African in Brodber's *Myal*.

17. The National Mento Yard highlights traditional folk forms in an affair in St. Ann Parish usually in October. For information on the various dance forms, see "Jamaica's Heritage in Dance," accessed April 8, 2021, https://jis.gov.jm /information/jamaicas-heritage-dance-music/jamaicas-heritage-dance/.

18. Pollard, *Homestretch*, 115.

19. Brodber, *Jane and Louisa*, 103–4. The folktale of Manalva apparently has Ghanaian origin. Mass Stanley seemed to associate the young Aunt Becca with Manalva. Manalva apparently was pretty and full of life, but foolish in her own way, as Aunt Becca was in her youth.

20. Brodber, *Jane and Louisa*, 104.

21. Schulenburg, "Identity and Dislocation in Caribbean Women's Literature: A Study of the Writings of Velma Pollard," MA Thesis, Cheltenham and Gloucester College of Higher Education, May 2001.

22. Pollard, *Homestretch*, 188.

23. Pollard, *Homestretch*, 181. The Jamaica Creole term "tallawah" suggests very tall in the sense of influence, spiritedness, etc.

24. Stefano Bellin, "Belonging and Unbelonging: Space, Identity, and Imagination," *Academia*, https://www.academia.edu/36774955/Belonging.

25. "Velma Pollard," unpublished interview with the author, Kingston, Jamaica, July 31, 2005. For the Shakespeare lines, see William Shakespeare, *The Merchant of Venice*, 4.1.15–35, in *The Complete Works*, ed. Stanley Wells and Gary Taylor, 2nd ed. (Oxford, UK: Clarendon Press, 2005), 471.

26. Anancy is a trickster mythological figure that was originally known mainly in Ghana in Africa, but was brought with enslaved persons to the Caribbean. For more information, see Chapter 3, note 18.

27. See Pollard, *Dread Talk: The Language of the Rastafari* (Kingston, Jamaica: Canoe Press, 2004).

28. Pollard, "Fly," *Crown Point and Other Poems* (London: Peepal Tree Press, 2003), 27. Some of this discussion of Pollard's poetry has been previously published in my article, Violet Harrington Bryan, "'Tomorrow's Spaces' in the Poetry of Jamaican Writer Velma Pollard," *Xavier Review* 33, no. 1 (Spring 2013): 49–52.

29. Pollard, *Considering Woman* (London: The Women's Press, 1989).

30. Pollard, "Anansa," *Crown Point*, 33.

31. See Edward Kamau Brathwaite, "Nation Language, History of the Voice: The Development of Nation Language in Anglophone Caribbean Poetry," in *The Post-Colonial Studies Reader*, 281–84; and Pollard, *Dread Talk*.

32. Bryan, "'Tomorrow's Spaces,'" 50.

33. Pollard, "Crown Point," *Crown Point*, 9.

34. Pollard, "Crown Point," *Crown Point*, 10.

35. Pollard, "Crown Point," *Crown Point*, 10.

36. Pollard, "Bud/Unbudded," *Crown Point*, 20.

37. "After Adowa," *Crown Point*, 39–40. The Ghanaian song and dance can be compared to the expression "Sammy dead," which is repeated often in Brodber's third novel, *Louisiana*. See Chapter 3 in this book.

38. Pollard, "Drake's Strait (from Virgin Islands Suite)," *Caribbean Quarterly* 38, nos. 2–3: vi–vii.

39. Pollard, "Drake's Strait Revisited," *Shame Trees Don't Grow Here . . . but Poincianas Bloom* (London: Peepal Tree Books, 1992), 12.

40. Pollard, "Drake's Strait Remembered," *Shame Trees*, 10–15.

41. There have been hurricanes that have sent thousands of refugees out to the US, Canada, and other parts of the Caribbean and South America, making the diaspora that had grown out of slavery a "new diaspora" in many varied parts of the world.

42. "Xunantunich," Part 2 of the poem "Belize Suite," *Crown Point and Other Poems* (London: Peepal Tree Press, 1988), 53.

43. "Launch of Velma Pollard's *And Caret Bay Again*," *The Jamaican Gleaner*, March 2013.

44. Pollard, "Caret Bay I," *Shame Trees*, 54.

45. Pollard, "Caret Bay," *And Caret Bay Again: New and Selected Poems* (London: Peepal Tree Press, 2013), 183.

46. For more information about the biography and politics of Rodney, see "Walter Rodney & Works," Walter Rodney Foundation, accessed July 7, 2017, http://www.walterrodneyfoundation.org/biography; and Horace G. Campbell, Presentation at the Africana Studies Research Center, African Colloquium Series, Cornell University, September 28, 2005. See also Chapters 1 and 2 of this book.

47. Walter Rodney, *How Europe Underdeveloped Africa* (London: Jessica and Eric Huntley of Bogle-L'Ouverture with Tanzanian Publishing House, 1972).

48. Pollard, "After Rodney," *Shame Trees*, 46–47.

49. Pollard, "After Rodney, I," *Shame Trees*, 46.

50. Pollard, "After Rodney, II," *Shame Trees*, 47.

51. Meredith M. Gadsby, *Sucking Salt: Caribbean Women Writers, Migration, and Survival* (Columbia: University of Missouri Press, 2006).

52. Pollard, "Cut Language," *Leaving Traces* (London: Peepal Tree Press, 2008), 41.

CHAPTER 5. ERNA BRODBER'S *THE RAINMAKER'S MISTAKE* AND *NOTHING'S MAT* AS AFROFUTURISTIC AND SPECULATIVE FICTION

1. Annie Neugebauer, "What Is Speculative Fiction?," March 24, 2014, annie bauer.com/2014/03/24/what-is-speculative-fiction?

2. Ytasha L. Womack, *Afrofuturism: The World of Black SciFi and Fantasy Culture* (Chicago: Chicago Review Press, 2013), 18.

3. Womack, *Afrofuturism*, 19, 82–83.

4. Elizabeth DeLoughrey, "Yam, Roots, and Rot: Allegories of the Provision Grounds," *Small Axe* 15, no. 1 (March 2011): 59.

5. Brodber, *The Rainmaker's Mistake* (London: New Beacon Books, 2007), 1–2. Citations to this novel are to this edition.

6. DeLoughrey, "Yam, Roots, and Rot," 58–75.

7. See DeLoughrey, "Yam, Roots, and Rot."

8. Brodber, *Rainmaker's Mistake*, 1.

9. Brodber, *Rainmaker's Mistake*, 1.

10. Brodber, *Rainmaker's Mistake*, 8.

11. Brodber, *Rainmaker's Mistake*, 1, 13.

12. Brodber, *Rainmaker's Mistake*, 1.

13. Brodber, *Rainmaker's Mistake*, 10.

14. Brodber, *Rainmaker's Mistake*, 11.

15. Brodber, *Rainmaker's Mistake*, 13.

16. Brodber, *Rainmaker's Mistake*, 13.

17. Brodber, *Rainmaker's Mistake*, 13.

18. Jamie Broadnax, "What the Heck Is Afrofuturism?," *Huffington Post*, February 16, 2018, huffingtonpost.com/entry/opinion-broadnax-afrofuturism -black-panther.

19. Steven Shapiro, "Review of *After Abolition: Britain and the Slave Trade Since 1807*," *Origins: Current Events in Historical Perspective*, July 2008, https:// origins.osu.edu/review/after-abolition-britain-and-slave-trade-1807.

20. Claudius K. Fergus, *Revolutionary Emancipation in the British West Indies* (Baton Rouge: Louisiana State University Press, 2013). Jamaica reluctantly makes history by freeing its enslaved persons.

21. Edouard Glissant, *Caribbean Discourse* (Charlottesville: University Press of Virginia, 1999), 69–92.

22. Brodber, *Rainmaker's Mistake*, 16.

23. Brodber, *Rainmaker's Mistake*, 20.

24. Brodber, *Rainmaker's Mistake*, 69.

25. See Kelly Josephs, *Beyond Geography, Past Time: Afrofuturism, The Rainmaker's Mistake, and Caribbean Studies* (Durham, NC: Duke University Press, 2013), 123–35; and Mark Dery, "Black to the Future: Interviews with Samuel R. Delany, Greg Tate, and Tricia Rose," in *Flame Wars: The Discourse of Cyberculture* (Durham, NC: Duke University Press, 1994), 180.

26. Josephs, *Beyond Geography*, 129.

27. Brodber, *Rainmaker's Mistake*, 28–29.

28. Brodber, *Rainmaker's Mistake*, 50–51.

29. Brodber, *Rainmaker's Mistake*, 57.

30. Brodber, *Rainmaker's Mistake*, 94.

31. See Cordelia Forbes, "Review of *The Rainmaker's Mistake* (2007)," *Postcolonial Text* 5, no. 3 (2009); and DeLoughrey, "Yam, Roots, and Rot."

32. Brodber, *Rainmaker's Mistake*, 125.

33. Brodber, *Rainmaker's Mistake*, 140.

34. Brodber, *Rainmaker's Mistake*, 138.

35. Brodber, *Rainmaker's Mistake*, 137.

36. Brodber, *Rainmaker's Mistake*, 150.

37. A fractal is defined as "an irregular geometric structure that cannot be described by classical geometry because magnification of the structure reveals repeated patterns of similarly irregular, but progressively smaller, dimensions" (accessed April 9, 2021, https://www.dictionary.com/browse/fractal).

38. See Neugebauer, "What Is Speculative Fiction?"

39. Brodber, *Nothing's Mat* (Kingston, Jamaica: University of the West Indies Press, 2014), 5. Citations to this novel are to this edition.

40. Brodber, *Nothing's Mat*, 7.

41. Shea Gunther, "14 Amazing Fractals Found in Nature," *Treehugger*, updated May 7, 2020, https://www.treehugger.com/amazing-fractals-found-in-nature -4868776.

42. Brodber, *Nothing's Mat*, 11.

43. Brodber, *Nothing's Mat*, 13.

44. Brodber, *Nothing's Mat*, 13–14.

45. Brodber, *Nothing's Mat*, 36.

46. Rebecca Romdhani, "Patterns of Loving: Erna Brodber's *Nothing's Mat*," *SX Salon: A Small Axe Literary Platform*, February 29, 2016.

47. The Morant Bay Rebellion of 1865 is discussed in Chapter 1.

48. Brodber, *Nothing's Mat*, 43.

49. Brodber, *Nothing's Mat*, 46.

50. Brodber, *Nothing's Mat*, 47.

51. Brodber, *Nothing's Mat*, 51. On the children of Israel, see Exodus 13:17–18.

52. Brodber, *Nothing's Mat*, 51.

53. Brodber, *Nothing's Mat*, 106.

CHAPTER 6. GENDER AND IDENTITY IN THE SHORT FICTION OF VELMA POLLARD AND ERNA BRODBER

1. Genonma Tang Nain and Barbara Bailey, *Gender Equality in the Caribbean: Reality and Illusion* (Kingston, Jamaica: Ian Randle Publishers, 2003).

2. Annelle Bellany, Alrjandro Hoyos, and Hugo Nopo, *Gender Earnings Gaps in the Caribbean: Evidence from Barbados and Jamaica* (Washington, DC: Inter-American Development Bank, August 2010).

3. Citations to these collections are to these editions: Pollard, *Considering Woman* (London: The Woman's Press, 1989); Pollard, *Karl and Other Stories* (London: Longman Group UK, 1994); and Pollard, *Considering Woman I & II* (Leeds, UK: Peeple Tree Press, 2010).

4. Pollard, "Cage II," *Considering Woman*, 15.

5. Jamaican independence occurred on July 19, 1962, when the British Parliament passed the Jamaica Independence Act, granting independence as of August 6, 1962; but it is often celebrated on August 1, along with the Emancipation Day recognition when enslaved persons were liberated in Jamaica and all the British Commonwealth countries.

6. Leith Dunn and Suzanne Scafe, "African-Caribbean Women: Migration, Diaspora, Post-Diaspora," *Caribbean Review of Gender Studies* 13 (2019): 1–16.

7. Pollard, "Orinthia, Is That You?," *Considering Woman I & II*, 88.

8. Pollard, "Orinthia, Is That You?," *Considering Woman I & II*, 88.

9. Pollard, "Sister I," *Considering Woman*, 24.

10. Pollard, "My Mother (for Marjorie)," *Considering Woman*, 30–31.

11. Maidenhair ferns are hardy plants but have a delicate appearance with bright green, thinly cut fronds with dark stalks and leaf shafts; they thrive best in the shade.

12. Pollard, "My Mother (for Marjorie)," *Considering Woman*, 32–33.

13. Pollard, "Georgia and Them There United States," *Karl and Other Stories*, 99.

14. Pollard, "Georgia," *Karl and Other Stories*, 99.

15. Gayatri Chakravorty Spivak, "Can the Subaltern Speak?," in *Colonial Discourse and Post-Colonial Theory: A Reader*, ed. Patrick Williams and Laura Chrisman (New York: Columbia University Press, 1994), 66–111.

16. Pollard, "A Night's Tale," *Karl and Other Stories*, 86.

17. Pollard, "Rainbow Corner," *Karl and Other Stories*, 93.

18. Pollard, "Rainbow Corner," *Karl and Other Stories*, 93.

19. Pollard, "The Americas in Anglophone Caribbean Women Writers: Bridges of Sound," *Changing English* 15, no. 2 (June 2008): 179–88.

20. Daryl Cumber Dance, "Conversations with Pam Mordecai and Velma Pollard," in *New World Adams; Conversations with Contemporary West Indian Writers* (London: Peepal Press, 1992), 184.

21. Pollard, "After Cages," *Leaving Traces* (London: Peepal Press, 2007), 30.

22. Pollard, "After Cages," *Leaving Traces*, 30.

23. Pollard, "After Cages," *Leaving Traces*, 31.

24. The following references to "Gran" are from the first collection in the edition specified.

25. Pollard, "Gran," *Considering Woman*, 34.

26. Pollard, "Gran," *Considering Woman*, 35–36.

27. Pollard, "Gran," *Considering Woman*, 37–38.

28. Pollard, "The Most Important Reason I Write," in *Caribbean Women Writers: Fiction in English*, ed. Maryse Conde and Thorunn Lonsdale (New York: Palgrave, 1999), 17–22.

29. Pollard, "Gran," *Considering Woman*, 40.

30. Pollard, "Gran," *Considering Woman*, 49.

31. Pollard, "Gran," *Considering Woman*, 49.

32. Pollard, "Gran," *Considering Woman*, 55–56.

33. Pollard, "Gran," *Considering Woman*, 65.

34. Pollard, "Gran," *Considering Woman*, 67.

35. Pollard, "Gran," *Considering Woman*, 69.

36. Brodber, *The World Is a High Hill: Stories about Jamaican Women* (Kingston, Jamaica: Ian Randle Press, 2012).

37. Brodber, "One Bubby Susan," in *The Penguin Book of Caribbean Short Stories*, ed. E. A. Markham (New York: Penguin Books, 1996), 48–53; Brodber, "Sleeping's Beauty and the Prince," in *Blue Latitudes: Caribbean Writers at Home and Abroad*, ed. Elizabeth Nunez and Jennifer Sparrow (Emeryville, CA, 2006), 27–31.

38. Evelyn Callaghan, "Play It Back a Next Way: Teaching Brodber Teaching Us," *Small Axe* 16: 59–71.

39. Atkinson, "Taino Influence on Jamaican Folk Tradition," *College of the Bahamas Research Journal* 12 (2011).

40. See Brodber, "Fiction in the Scientific Procedure," in *Caribbean Women Writers: Essays from the First International Conference*, ed. Selwyn R. Cudjoe (Wellesley, MA: Callalouxx Publications, 1990); and Deborah Plant, *Every Tub Must Sit on Its Own Bottom: The Philosophy and Politics of Zora Neale Hurston* (Champaign: University of Illinois Press, 1995).

41. Pollard discusses the Jamaica Creole continuum of Jamaican language in her *Dread Talk* (Montreal: McGill-Queen's University Press, 2000), 4–24.

42. Brodber, "One Bubby Susan," *Penguin Book of Caribbean Short Stories*, 49. The term "rat-bat" is a term of Standard English that refers to a type of bat-like creature that habitually resides in tall ceilings, such as church steeples. The term is also a folk term of Jamaican Creole, which suggests a busy creature that moves around quickly and disturbs people, as houseflies, gnats, or mosquitoes do. The term is used often in Brodber's and Pollard's work, as in Brodber's *Jane and Louisa*, Pollard's *Homestretch*, and the stories of both writers.

43. See Helen Tiffin, "Cold Hearts and Foreign Tongues: Recitation and Reclamation of the Female Body in the Work of Erna Brodber and Jamaica Kincaid," *Callaloo* 16, no. 4 (Autumn 1993): 911.

44. Asantehene was mythically and historically the oldest king of the Ashanti people, and his home capital was in Kumasi of Ghana. The capital was the point of departure for many Africans who were part of the Atlantic slave trade.

45. Marcus Garvey is a Jamaican hero. See Chapters 1 and 3 of this book.

46. Romdhani, "Patterns of Loving: Erna Brodber's *Nothing's Mat,*" *SX Salon: A Small Axe Literary Platform*, February 29, 2016.

47. Carolyn Cooper, "An Interview," in Brodber, *World Is a High Hill*, 177–79.

48. Cooper, "Interview," in Brodber, *World Is a High Hill*, 183.

49. Shepherd, "Foreword," in Brodber, *World Is a High Hill*, xiii.

50. Pollard, Interview, 12th International Conference of the Short Story (Arkansas), 2012; and Pollard, "Most Important Reason."

51. Pollard, "The Americas."

52. Pollard, *Dread Talk*, 83–85.

53. Pollard, *Anansesem: A Collection of Caribbean Folk Tales, Legends, and Poems for Juniors* (Kingston, Jamaica: Longman Jamaica, 1985).

54. See Horace G. Campbell. "Walter Rodney and Pan-Africanism Today," Lecture, African Americana Studies, Cornell University July 28, 2005. Also, see Chapters 1 and 2 in this book.

55. For more information, see Daryl Cumber Dance, "Go Eena Kumbls: A Comparison of Erna Brodber's *Jane and Louisa Will Soon Come Home* and Toni Cade Bambara's *The Salt Eaters*," in Cudjoe, *Caribbean Women Writers*, 69–186.

56. The first conference was on "Regenerating the Black Poetic Tradition," held in 1997; the second was on "Seeding the Future of American Poetry," held in 2014 at James Madison University.

57. James, "Five Jamaican Novels You Should Read: Shape-Shifters, Metafictions, and a Whole Lot of Sex," *Literary Hub*, September 30, 2015, https://lithub.com/marlon-james-five-jamaican-novels-you-should-read/.

58. Jia Tolentino, "Why Marlon James Decided to Write an African 'Game of Thrones,'" *New Yorker*, January 28, 2019.

INDEX

abolition of slavery, 84–85, 96, 125n11;
  Slavery Abolition Act, 13
Abraham, Keshia, 18
activism, 34, 53, 59; Erna Brodber and,
  5; Walter Rodney and, 78
Adowa, 75
African Americans, 53, 59, 64, 71, 80;
  Black Atlantic, 64; Black consciousness, 6, 17; Black intellectuals, 33;
  Black Jamaicans, 15–18; Black literature, 117–18; Black nationalism,
  110, 116; Black Power movement,
  8, 22, 98, 123n50; colonialism and,
  15, 96; in *Jane and Louisa*, 33–34,
  36–37; in *Karl*, 25, 29; and literature, 114–15; in *Louisiana*, 39, 59,
  63. *See also* Afrofuturism
African diaspora: Blackspace, 18; consciousness, 57, 125; Erna Brodber
  and, 18; literature, 3; in *Louisiana*,
  54, 55, 62; Marcus Garvey and, 59,
  64; in *Myal*, 47–50; new African
  Jamaican, 66, 68, 71, 74–75, 79,
  92; in *Nothing's Mat*, 92, 96; Pan-
  Africanism, 23, 59, 64, 78, 126n28;
  in *The Rainmaker's Mistake*, 81–82;
  the sisters and, 4–6, 11, 16, 22, 100,
  114–15, 117; and spiritual practices,
  14, 31, 39, 45, 48, 50, 53, 55, 82, 114;
  Velma Pollard and, 64, 68, 74–75,
  79, 102
Afrofuturism, 80, 110; Erna Brodber
  and, 5, 20; in *Nothing's Mat*, 93;

  in *The Rainmaker's Mistake*, 85,
  87, 93
*Afrofuturism: The World of Black SciFi
  and Fantasy Culture*, 80
"After Adowa" (Velma Pollard), 75
"After Cages" (Velma Pollard), 106
"After Rodney" (Velma Pollard), 78
allegories, 11, 30, 33, 48, 111, 113; African
  Americans and, 53, 59, 64, 71, 80,
  114–15
American Revolution, 13
Anancy, 115–16, 124n60; Erna Brodber
  and, 34–35, 45, 60, 62, 115–16; in
  *Jane and Louisa Will Soon Come
  Home*, 34–35; in *Louisiana*, 60, 62;
  in *Myal*, 45; tale of Anancy and
  Dryhead, 35; Velma Pollard and,
  4, 7, 10, 72, 73, 115–16
*Anansesem: A Collection of Caribbean
  Folk Tales, Legends, and Poems for
  Juniors* (Velma Pollard), 4, 10, 116
ancestors: bonds with, 14; Erna Brodber
  and, 18; in *Jane and Louisa Will
  Soon Come Home*, 30, 32–33, 35,
  37–38; in *Louisiana*, 55–57; in *Noth-
  ing's Mat*, 81, 92–93, 96, 99; in *The
  Rainmaker's Mistake*, 82; spirits,
  42, 48–50, 82, 90, 99; Velma Pollard and, 75
*And Caret Bay Again: New and Selected
  Poems* (Velma Pollard), 4, 77
Anglican church, 12, 19, 30, 67, 74, 114,
  122n35

anthropology: Erna Brodber and, 4–5,
9, 11, 109, 127n54; in *Louisiana*,
52–53, 55, 59; in "One Bubby Susan,"
109
apprentices, 13, 84–85, 124n64
Arawak people, 11, 76, 109–11
Ashanti people, 45, 77, 124, 126n18,
126n29; and Asantehene, 110,
135n44
Atkinson, Lesley-Gail, 109
Atlantic crossings, 13, 76
Atlantic slave trade, 11, 92, 115, 135n44

Babylon, 26–27, 38, 122n27
"Bagnolds District of St. Mary, Jamaica
and the Atlantic Crossings of the
Late Eighteenth Century, The"
(Erna Brodber), 13
Baptist Church, 15, 31, 47, 49, 67
Barrett, Leonard, 121n3
Beckford, George, 32–33
Belize, 10, 65, 74–77, 114
"Belize Suite" (Velma Pollard), 76
Bellin, Stefano, 71, 130n24
belonging, 72; "unbelonging," 4, 65
Best, Lloyd, 32–33
*Best Philosophers I Know Can't Read or
Write, The* (Velma Pollard), 4, 25
Bhabha, Homi, 44
Bible, 20, 42, 61, 74; allegory in, 48; New
Testament, 61; Old Testament,
61, 110
bildungsroman, 24, 121n7
biracial people, 40, 44, 49, 98–99, 125n8;
marriages, 14; "silver," 98
Blackspace, 5–6, 18
Boer Wars, 16, 74, 108
"border crossing," 112
Brathwaite, Edward Kamau, 5, 10, 74
Brodber, Erna: awards of, 5, 117; back-
ground of, 3–4; at Gettysburg Col-
lege, 11; and intellectual work, 4, 8;

and Jamaican history, 6–9, 11, 13,
16–19, 116; literary reception of,
5–6, 117–18; narrative style of, 14,
20–21, 24, 36, 115; and religion, 15;
short fiction of, 108–13; and sociology, 6, 8–9, 128n70; and women,
115
Works: *Abandonment of Children in
Jamaica*, 8; "The Bagnolds District
of St. Mary, Jamaica," 13; "Fiction
in the Scientific Procedure," 8;
"Kishwana," 112, 115–16; *Nothing's
Mat*, 4–5, 14, 80–81, 92–99, 114;
"One Bubby Susan," 108–9, 113,
115; *The People of My Jamaican
Village, 1817–1948*, 6, 19; *The Rainmaker's Mistake*, vii, 5, 13–14, 81–
92, 93, 99; "Rosa," 111–12, 116; *The
Second Generation of Freemen
in Jamaica, 1907–1944*, 6, 8, 13;
"Sleeping's Beauty and a Prince
Charming," 108, 110–11, 113; *Wood-
side, Pear Tree Grove P.O.*, 6, 11,
13–15, 18; *The World Is a High Hill*,
5, 100, 111–13; "Writing Your Vil-
lage History—the Case of Wood-
side," 6, 12; *Yards in the City of
Kingston*, 8. See also *Jane and
Louisa Will Soon Come Home*;
Louisiana; *Myal*
Brodber, Ernest, 3
Brodber, Lucy, 3
Bruckins Musical Group, 69–70
Bryan, Violet Harrington, 121n35, 130n35
Bustamante, Alexander, 17, 121n4
Butler, Octavia, 80, 118

"Cages" (Velma Pollard), 73, 101, 106
callaloo plant, 80–82, 94, 115
Canada, 9–10, 14, 16, 64–65, 78–79, 113;
in *Karl*, 24–26, 30
capitalism, 8, 22, 82, 102

Caribbean: Anglophone writers in, 74, 115; Erna Brodber and, 18, 85; in *Jane and Louisa Soon Will Come Home*, 32–33; in *Louisiana*, 56–57; the sisters and, 3–5, 10–11, 20, 113–16; Velma Pollard and, 9–10, 64, 75–78, 103; writers from, 5, 8, 27, 74

Casa de las Americas, 10, 23

Castro, Anne Margaret, 39

Castro, Fidel, 22

Chevannes, Barry, 121n3, 123n27

Chicago, Illinois, 40, 53–54, 60, 62–63

Christianity, 15, 41, 48, 95, 107; Anglican church, 12, 19, 30, 67, 74, 114, 122n35; Baptist church, 15, 31, 47, 49, 67

churches, 28, 54, 67–68; Anglican church, 12, 19, 30, 67, 74, 114, 122n35; Baptist church, 15, 31, 47, 49, 67; fundamentalist, 31; and hymnals, 30; Jehovah's Witnesses, 67; Methodist, 15, 43–45, 47–49, 52, 67; Pentecostal, 67; Seventh-Day Adventist, 67

civil rights movement, 22, 98

class, 16, 24, 26, 44, 102; middle, 8, 28, 112; women and, 101, 103; working, 78, 101, 113

Cobham, Rhonda, 31

"Colon Man" myth, 16

colonialism: British, 13, 75, 77–78, 84, 125n11; in Jamaica, 15–17, 19, 38, 116; in *Myal*, 42–43, 50; neocolonialism, 17, 23, 24, 26; in *Nothing's Mat*, 96; postcolonialism, ix, 5, 17, 42, 99, 110; in *The Rainmaker's Mistake*, 89; and sisters' identities, 10

Columbia University, 7, 52, 59

Comfort Hall (Jamaica), 68, 107–8

commonwealth countries, British, 5, 10, 36, 67, 77, 84, 93; emancipation in, 102, 134n5

community life, traditions of, 57, 75; Erna Brodber and, 18, 32, 38, 111–

12, 116; in *Homestretch*, 66–67; in *Louisiana*, 56; in *Nothing's Mat*, 96, 99; sisters' parents and, 7; and spiritual theft, 50; Velma Pollard and, 72, 74, 106, 116

Considering Woman (Velma Pollard), 73, 101, 103, 106, 112, 115

Considering Woman I & II: New and Selected Stories (Velma Pollard), 4, 100–101, 103, 106

Cooper, Carolyn, 111–12

Cowan, David, 67

Creole language, 7, 9, 25–27, 41, 56, 71–74, 79, 97, 109

creolization, 6, 11

Crown Point and Other Poems (Velma Pollard), 4, 20, 73–74

Cryderman, Kevin Arthur, "The Language of *Jane and Louisa*," 32

Cuba, 10, 16, 22, 30, 74, 102

culture: African diaspora and, 16–18, 22, 64, 74–75; colonialism and, 77; diversity of, 44; folklore and, 63, 68–69, 79, 117; food and, 82; Ghanaian Jamaican, 8; history of, 71; hybridity and, 43–44; immigration and, 13, 15; Jamaican postindependence, 30; music and, 56–57; Rastafarian, 28; rural Jamaican, 113; sisters and, 3–4, 9, 20, 100, 113; theory of, 11, 80, 113–14; West African, 4, 113

"Cut Language" (Velma Pollard), 79

Dagninini, Jeremie Krubo, 128n64

Dance, Daryl Cumber, 34, 106, 120n12, 120n13, 123n52, 124n57, 134n20, 136n55

dancing, 25, 35, 69, 97; Adowa, 75; Horsehead Maypole, 69; Johnkunnu, 69; Myal, 41, 49–50; quadrille, 69, 77; second line, 75; sword, 70

D'Costa, Jean, 10
death: in *Considering Woman*, 108; funerals, 56, 60, 75, 97; in *Jane and Louisa Will Soon Come Home*, 31; in *Louisiana*, 52–57, 60–62; in *The Rainmaker's Mistake*, 89–90; "Sammy Dead," 75, 128n62, 131n37; spiritual practices and, 4, 15, 52–57, 60–62, 75, 114; of Walter Rodney, 78
Dekker, Desmond, and the Specials, 128n62
Delaney, Martin, 64
Delany, Samuel, 80, 118
DeLoughrey, Elizabeth, 82
Dery, Mark, 80
diaspora, African. *See* African diaspora
dislocation, 5, 70, 72, 103–4
diversity, 11, 15, 43–44, 64, 111, 125n10
Donnell, Allison, 5
Doumerc, Eric, 27
"Drake" (Velma Pollard), 75
Drake, Sir Francis, 76
"Drake's Strait Remembered" (Velma Pollard), 76
"Drake's Strait Revisited" (Velma Pollard), 76
Dread Talk, 26, 72, 79
Dread Talk: The Language of the Rastafari (Velma Pollard), 4, 8, 10, 26–27, 39, 115
Du Bois, W. E. B., 64, 118
dub poetry, 27, 115
Dunn, Leith, 64

economy: Institute of Social and Economic Research, 6, 8; International Monetary Fund, 22; of Jamaica, 17, 19, 38, 102, 116; Marcus Garvey and, 16
education: in *Homestretch*, 70–71; in Jamaica, 16, 18, 22, 46, 50, 52, 64;

in *Karl*, 26, 28; in *Myal*, 42–43, 46, 50, 52; of Velma Pollard, 4, 7, 100
Edward, Brent Hayes, 64
emancipation, 6, 127n42; Emancipation Day, 18, 69, 102, 134n5; Erna Brodber on, 13–15, 19, 81; and freed persons, 13–15, 81, 84–86, 96, 99, 111, 116, 124n64; in *The Rainmaker's Mistake*, 81, 84–86, 91–92
employment opportunities, 16, 28, 100, 105
England: emigration to, 12, 25, 44, 79; in *Homestretch*, 65–69, 71; London in, 7, 66, 85–86, 88, 90–93; in *Nothing's Mat*, 93–95; Rastafarianism in, 30; travelers from, 11; Velma Pollard and, 3, 9–10, 76–77. *See also* Great Britain
English language, 23, 78, 79; Jamaican Creole, 26, 74, 76, 79
estates, 12–15, 19, 52, 95
Ethiopia, 17, 23
ethnicities, 18, 44, 92, 102
ethnographies, 5–6, 11, 55
Europe, 11, 30, 43; and colonization, 47, 75, 78, 82, 126n29; eurocentrism, 89; European folktales, 110–11; and slavery, 91
Evans, Bill, "Tacky's Slave Rebellion," 47, 126n31

family of Brodber and Pollard, 7, 20, 115–16; and "cages," 10; in *Considering Woman*, 106, 108; Erna Brodber on, 111; history, 33, 80–81, 94; in *Jane and Louisa Will Soon Come Home*, 30–33, 35–38; in *Myal*, 45; in *Nothing's Mat*, 81, 92–99; in Velma Pollard's poetry, 74–75, 79; in Woodside, 13, 18
fantasy, 80, 87, 115
Fernandez-Omos, Margarite, 41

fiction, 3, 15, 100–101, 113–16; Afrofuturism, 20, 80, 93, 110; of Erna
Brodber, 6, 8–9, 13, 20, 48, 80, 85,
87, 93; and history, 85; interdisciplinary, 5, 108; magical realism,
87; mimetic, 80; postcolonial, 5;
realistic, 70, 80, 93, 111; science fiction, 80; speculative, 5, 13, 20, 80,
87, 92–93, 118; of Velma Pollard,
9–10, 20, 23, 64–65, 79, 101, 107–8
"Fiction in the Scientific Procedure"
(Erna Brodber), 8
"Fly" (Velma Pollard), 7, 73, 115
folklore, ix, 5, 19–20, 113; African, 4–5,
23, 115–17, 126n18; Caribbean, 4–5,
10; Erna Brodber and, 13, 26, 109;
folk culture, 79, 113; folk religion,
45; folk songs, 55–57, 128n62; folktales, 110–11, 130n19; in *Louisiana*,
55, 63; Rastafarianism and, 23;
Velma Pollard and, 10, 68–69,
73–74
food, 13, 82, 102
Founder's Day, 83
fractals, 92, 93–95, 98, 133n37
freedom, 15, 67, 101–2; and freed persons, 13–15, 81, 84–86, 96, 99, 111,
116, 124n64
funeral dances, 75
Furious Flower conferences, 114, 117

Gabbin, Joanne, 117
Gadsby, Meredith, 78
Garvey, Marcus, 16–17, 23, 40, 64, 110,
116, 126n28; Garveyites, 17, 40, 62;
in *Karl*, 47; and longshoremen's
strike, 17, 53–54, 62; in *Louisiana*,
53, 56, 59–60, 62
gender: equality, 100; feminism, 9; men,
16, 41, 50, 97–98, 100–101, 103, 105,
116; patriarchy, 21, 101, 103, 111, 115–
16. *See also* women

"Genosuicide," 91
"Georgia and Them There United
States" (Velma Pollard), 104
Gettysburg College, 11
Ghana, 4, 8, 75, 82, 116, 124n60, 126n29,
130n19, 135n44
Gilroy, Paul, 64
Girvan, Norman, 32
Glissant, Edouard, 85
"Gran" (Velma Pollard), 106–8
Great Britain: and abolition of slavery,
13, 85, 102, 125n11; and Boer Wars,
16; British Virgin Islands, 10, 74;
and colonialism, 12–14, 52, 75–77;
and diaspora, 66, 81; and immigration, 14, 66; Jamaican independence from, ix, 13, 42, 102, 134n5;
literature, 7, 46, 90; Marcus Garvey
and, 17; in *Myal*, 44, 49; in *Nothing's Mat*, 92, 95; and slavery, 85,
110. *See also* commonwealth countries: British; England
Grenada, 74–75
Guyana, 10, 75, 78

Hall, Stuart, 11, 64
Harlem Renaissance, 51
healers, 30, 34, 47, 89
Hibbert, Toots, 23
history: cultural, 71; of diaspora, 64,
115; Erna Brodber and, 4–9, 11–20,
80–81, 108–9, 111, 116; family, 33,
80–81, 94; historiography, 96, 102;
in *Homestretch*, 71; in *Jane and
Louisa Will Soon Come Home*,
33, 36; in *Louisiana*, 52, 59–60; in
Myal, 47, 50; in *Nothing's Mat*, 92–
93, 96; in *The Rainmaker's Mistake*, 85; social, 60; Velma Pollard
and, 19–20, 71, 76–77, 107, 116;
women and, 100; of Woodside,
4, 11–19

Homestretch (Velma Pollard), 4, 7, 9–10,
    20, 65–66, 69–72, 79, 114, 117
hoodoo, 9, 15, 39, 50, 52–53, 55, 57, 61,
    128n61
housing, 13, 22, 34
Howard University, 98
hurricanes, 15–16, 74, 76, 131n41
Hurston, Zora Neale, 9, 51, 53, 109,
    135n40
hybridity, 11, 42–44, 64, 125n8, 125n10

identity: Caribbean, 10–11; diaspora, 11;
    in Erna Brodber's short stories,
    111, 116; Jamaican, 30, 79; Jamaican
    women and, 21; in *Jane and Louisa*,
    32–33; kumbla, 36–37; in *Nothing's
    Mat*, 94–95; in *The Rainmaker's
    Mistake*, 87; in Velma Pollard's
    short stories, 100, 101, 116
immigration, 13, 45, 69, 127n42
indentured servants, 11, 13, 92, 96–97,
    115, 127n42
independence, Jamaican, ix, 17–18; and
    Caribbean identity, 10; in *Jane and
    Louisa Will Soon Come Home*,
    30, 33, 38; post, 22–24, 28, 102; in
    Velma Pollard's poetry, 78; women
    and, 9
indigenous people, 76, 109; Arawak,
    11, 76, 109–11; Ashanti, 45, 77, 124,
    126n18, 126n29; Igbo, 82; Mayan,
    76; Taino, 11, 19, 76, 109
Institute of Social and Economic Re-
    search (ISER), 6, 8
intellectual work: Erna Brodber and, 4,
    8; movements, 30, 33–34
interdisciplinary fiction, 5, 108
International Monetary Fund (IMF), 22
Ireland, 11; Irish character in *Myal*, 40,
    44–45
Israel, Kingdom of, 29, 48, 98, 126n33

Jamaica: Kingston in, 3, 6–8, 16, 25–28,
    71–72, 99, 100, 112; Labour Party
    in, 17; St. Catherine Parish in, 3, 74;
    St. Thomas Parish, 12, 40, 49, 77, 96;
    Xaymaca, 109. *See also* indepen-
    dence, Jamaican; St. Mary's Parish,
    Jamaica; Woodside, Jamaica
James, Marlon, 117, 136nn57–58
Jane and Louisa Will Soon Come Home
    (Erna Brodber), 4–5, 8, 22, 25,
    30–38; belonging in, 72; creative
    postcolonialism in, ix; female sex-
    uality in, 95; folklore in, 115; the
    Manalva in, 70; Marcus Garvey
    in, 17; metaphor in, 58; narrative
    technique of, 24, 114; spirituality
    in, 9, 15
Jerry, Bongo, 27
John, Catherine, 18
Josephs, Kelly, 87–88
Judeo-Christian religion, 41, 48

Karl (Velma Pollard), 10, 20, 22, 23–30,
    38, 46; capitalism in, 8; migration
    in, 9; Rastafari cosmogeny in, 39
Karl and Other Stories (Velma Pollard),
    101, 105
Kenya, 66, 117, 129n6
Kingston, Jamaica, 3, 6–8, 16, 25–28,
    71–72, 99, 100, 112
Kipling, Rudyard, 43, 46, 125n11
"Kishwana" (Erna Brodber), 112, 115–16
Kortenaar, Neil Ten, 119n1, 125n6,
    127n36
kumbla, the, 30–38, 79, 116
Kumina religion, 4, 39, 45–47, 49–50,
    55, 69

labor: enslaved, 13–15, 82–84; factories,
    66–67; freed, 15, 84; Jamaica's La-
    bour Party, 17; and the Panama

Canal, 121n8; in *The Rainmaker's Mistake*, 81–84, 87, 89–91

language, 4, 5, 9, 114–15; Creole, 7, 9, 25–27, 41, 56, 71–74, 79, 97, 109; Dread Talk, 8, 26, 72, 79; in *Karl*, 23, 26–27; nation, 74, 79; patois, 74, 79; studies of, 4, 72–73; in Velma Pollard's poetry, 72–74, 79. *See also* English language; linguistic ritual

Laveau, Marie, 128n61

Leaving Traces (Velma Pollard), 4, 79

Lebanese immigrants, 15, 45

liberation movements: African, 8; Black, 116; Jamaican Liberation Day, 102; women's, 8

linear narratives, 8, 24, 69–79, 112

linguistic ritual, 44, 125n15

literary studies, 4–5, 10–11, 14, 33, 78, 110, 117

literature: African American, 114–15; British, 7; Caribbean, 115, 117; diasporic, 3, 64; history and, 85; magical realism, 87; in *Nothing's Mat*, 95; sisters' parents and, 72; studies of, 4–5, 10–11, 14, 33, 78, 110, 117; Velma Pollard and, 9, 115

London, England, 7, 66, 85–86, 88, 90–93

longshoremen's strike, 17, 53–54, 62

Louisiana (Erna Brodber), 5, 20, 52–63, 75–76, 111, 114–15; Marcus Garvey in, 17, 40; religion in, 15; spirit possession in, 39, 53–54, 61

Louisiana (US state), 58–59, 62, 113; New Orleans, 15, 40, 53, 55–56, 58, 62–63, 75, 105, 113–14, 128n61

Louisiana area (Jamaica), 12, 52–53, 58–59, 62

love, 25, 48, 62, 67, 77, 89, 106–8; "antilove" stories, 10

"Mabrak" (Bongo Jerry), 27

magical realism, 87

Man Booker Prize, 117

Manalva, 69–70, 97, 130n19

Manley, Michael, 22, 30, 121n3

Manuel, Peter, 120n14, 122n13

Marley, Bob, 8, 22–23, 25, 30, 121n3; Marley and the Wailers, 8

marriage: biracial, 14; as a cage, 73, 115; in *Jane and Louisa Will Soon Come Home*, 36–37; in *Myal*, 48; in *Nothing's Mat*, 95, 98; in Velma Pollard's work, 73, 101, 105–6, 115

Marshall, Paule, 115

McAllister, Jared, 121n9

McGill University, 7

memories, 3, 5; cultural, 56; in *Louisiana*, 54–56, 58–59; in *The Rainmaker's Mistake*, 91; spirits and, 49, 54; in Velma Pollard's poetry, 74, 77, 107

men, 16, 41, 50, 97–98, 100–101, 103, 105, 116

mental health, 26, 28–30, 33–34

mento music, 25, 35, 56, 69–70, 62n28

metaphors, 11, 30, 37, 52, 56, 58, 76, 82

Methodist Church, 15, 43–45, 47–49, 52, 67

middle class, 8, 28, 112

migration: in Erna Brodber's writing, 13, 79, 100, 113; from Jamaica, 16; in Velma Pollard's writing, 4, 9, 64, 66, 100, 104–5

Monroe, Trevor, 32

Morant Bay, 12, 42, 44, 50, 92, 96–98; Morant Bay Rebellion, 36, 96, 116, 124n65

Mordecai, Pamela, 106

Morris, Mervyn, 27, 122n25

music: and Afrofuturism, 80; in *Homestretch*, 68–70; Jamaican, 10, 13, 22–23, 30, 113, 115–16; in *Louisiana*,

56; mento, 25, 35, 56, 69–70, 62n28; in *Myal*, 46, 50; reggae, 8, 22–23, 25, 30, 121n3

"My Mother (for Marjorie)" (Velma Pollard), 104, 116

Myal (Erna Brodber), ix, 5, 20, 39, 40–52, 53, 63, 108; belonging in, 72; reception of, 117; syncretic religion in, 15; timelessness in, 14; West African culture in, 4, 82

Myal (religion), 4, 39, 42, 50, 55, 125n10

mystical ideas, 20, 52–53, 59, 75, 127n52

myths, ix, 69, 90, 100, 108, 113, 115, 130n26, 135n44; of the "Colon Man," 16; creation, 81; foundation, 12; religious, 6

Nain, Genonma Tang, 100

narrative: of Erna Brodber, 14, 24, 36; in *Homestretch*, 69–70; linear, 8, 24, 69–79, 112; in *Louisiana*, 55, 57; narration, 44, 101; in *The Rainmaker's Mistake*, 14, 82–83, 87; of sisters, 3–4, 9, 24, 113–14, 117; of Velma Pollard, 24, 102

nation language, 74, 79

Neilson, John, 12

neocolonialism, 17, 23–24, 26

Neugebauer, Annie, 80

new African Jamaican diaspora, 66, 68, 71, 74–75, 79, 92

New Orleans, Louisiana, 15, 40, 53, 55–56, 58, 62–63, 75, 105, 113–14, 128n61

New York, New York, 45, 52, 54, 58–59, 102–4

nonfiction, 3, 10, 20, 44, 64, 114

nostalgia, 4, 65

Nothing's Mat (Erna Brodber), 4–5, 14, 80–81, 92–99, 114

Obeah, 4, 55, 123n45, 127n38; in *Jane and Louisa Will Soon Come Home*,

31, 34, 66; in *Karl*, 28; in *Myal*, 15, 39, 41, 46–47, 49–51

O'Callaghan, Evelyn, 7, 33, 108

occult practices, 41, 127n52

"On My Way to Somewhere, Of Course" (Velma Pollard), 103

"One Bubby Susan" (Erna Brodber), 108–9, 113, 115

oppression: of Black people, 78, 102, 103, 116; of women, 10, 100, 103, 116

oral discourse, ix, 5, 60; histories, 11; tradition, 27, 53, 74

"Orinthia, Is That You?" (Velma Pollard), 102–3

Osbey, Brenda Marie, 55, 128n60

"Our Mother" (Velma Pollard), 20

Pan-Africanism, 23, 59, 64, 78, 126n28

Panama, 16, 81, 92, 95

Panama Canal, 16, 24–25, 98, 121n8

Paravisini-Gerbert, Lizabeth, 41

patois, 74, 79

patriarchy, 21, 101, 103, 111, 115–16

Patterson, Orlando, 5

People of My Jamaican Village, 1817–1948, The (Erna Brodber), 6, 19

People's Nationalist Party (PNP), 22

philosophy, 25, 27, 74

piracy, 76–77, 85

place, ix, 3, 9, 68, 77, 87, 100, 114

plantations, 19, 47, 61, 81–84, 87, 91; coffee, 6, 11–12

poetry, 27, 43, 46, 55, 90, 106; dub, 27, 115; of Erna Brodber, 35; sisters', 3, 15, 113, 114–16; of Velma Pollard, ix, 4, 9–10, 20, 64–65, 67, 72–79, 101, 116–17

politics: of colonialism, 5; and diaspora, 64; political activism, 5, 33–34, 53, 59, 78; and postcolonialism, 42, 102; in Velma Pollard's poetry, 74–75

Pollard, Velma: background of, 3–4, 7–9; and "anti-love" stories, 10; and "Bitter Tales," 103; and genres, 20–21, 100–101, 115; and Jamaican history, 16–17, 116–17; Lifetime Achievement Award of, 117; literary reception of, 4–5, 117–18; and marriage as cage, 10, 115; and migration, 9–11, 64–65; pedagogical works by, 4, 10; poetry of, 4, 9–10, 20, 64–65, 67, 72–79, 101, 116–17; short fiction by, 101–8

Works: "After Adowa," 75; "After Cages," 106; "After Rodney," 78; *Anansesem: A Collection of Caribbean Folk Tales, Legends, and Poems for Juniors,* 4, 10, 116; *The Best Philosophers I Know Can't Read or Write,* 4, 25; *And Caret Bay Again: New and Selected Poems,* 4, 77; "Belize Suite," 76; "Cages," 73, 101, 106; *Considering Woman,* 73, 101, 103, 106, 112, 115; *Considering Woman I & II: New and Selected Stories,* 4, 100–101, 103, 106; *Crown Point and Other Poems,* 4, 20, 73–74; "Cut Language," 79; "Drake," 75; "Drake's Strait Remembered," 76; "Drake's Strait Revisited," 76; "Fly," 7, 73, 115; "Gran," 106–8; *Homestretch,* 4, 7, 9–10, 20, 65–66, 69–72, 79, 114, 117; *Karl and Other Stories,* 101, 105; *Leaving Traces,* 4, 79; "My Mother (for Marjorie)," 104, 116; "A Night's Tale," 105; "On My Way to Somewhere, Of Course," 103; "Orinthia, Is That You?," 102–3; "Our Mother," 20; "Rainbow Corner," 105; "Sea Wall," 76; *Shame Trees Don't Grow Here,* 4, 77–78; "Sister I," 103; "Virgin Island Suite,"

75; "Xunantunich," 76–77. See also *Karl* (Velma Pollard)

postcolonialism, ix, 5, 17, 42, 99, 110

poverty, 22, 28, 102, 112, 116

pregnancy, 31, 40, 58, 62, 70, 94, 103

property ownership, 12, 14, 28, 76, 96, 106, 111–12

proprietors, 12, 14–15, 32

quadrille dance, 69, 77

Queen Victoria, 35–36, 125n11

race, 16, 45, 98; biracial characters, 40, 44, 49, 98–99, 125n8; biracial marriages, 14; color, 26, 45, 101; mulatto, 45. *See also* African Americans; African diaspora

Rahming, Melvin B., 50, 119n1, 127n41

"Rainbow Corner" (Velma Pollard), 105

Rainmaker's Mistake, The (Erna Brodber), vii, 5, 13–14, 81–92, 93, 99

Randolph-Macon College, 11

rape, 40, 95, 97, 127n38

Rastafarians, 8, 17, 22–23, 25, 26–30, 32–33, 38; and *Dread Talk,* 4, 10, 39, 72

redemption, 17, 30, 38, 56

reggae, 8, 22–23, 25, 30, 121n3

religion, 83, 106; African-derived, 39, 45, 47, 55, 66, 113; Caribbean, 3–4, 6, 9, 27; Judeo-Christian religion, 41, 48; Kumina religion, 4, 39, 45–47, 49–50, 55, 69; Myal, 4, 39, 42, 50, 55, 125n10; mystical ideas, 20, 52–53, 59, 75, 127n52; ritual, 41, 125n10, 127n38; syncretic, 15, 48; voodoo, 9, 15, 39, 50, 52–53, 55, 57, 61, 128n61. *See also* Christianity; churches; Obeah; spirits

resistance, 4, 17, 50, 59, 62, 77, 89, 100, 110, 116

revolutionaries, 22, 29, 33, 78

Roberts, June E., 5, 32–33, 36, 51, 60

Rodney, Walter, 78, 116

Romdhani, Rebecca, 95, 111

"Rosa" (Erna Brodber), 111–12, 116

rural areas: Caribbean, 4; in *Consider-ing Woman*, 101, 103–4, 106, 112; in *Homestretch*, 65, 114; of Jamaica, 3, 7, 9, 15, 19–20, 116, 125n8, 125n10; in *Jane and Louisa Will Soon Come Home*, 15, 31; in *Karl*, 24–25, 27–28; in *Myal*, 40; in *Nothing's Mat*, 98–99; in Velma Pollard's poetry, 74; in *The World Is a High Hill*, 111, 113

Sairsingh, Marie, 14

"Sammy Dead" (song), 54, 56–57, 61, 75, 128n62, 131n37

Samuel, Petal, 33

Scafe, Suzanne, 64

scholarship: literary, 3–5, 9, 14, 74, 110, 117; of Velma Pollard, 72; of Walter Rodney, 78

Schulenberg, Darlene, 70

Scott, Dennis, 67

"Sea Wall" (Velma Pollard), 76

Second Generation of Freemen in Jamaica, 1907–1944, The (Erna Brodber), 6, 8, 13

Selassie, Haile, 17, 23, 29

sexuality, 24, 39, 45, 89–90, 103; female, 95, 101, 111; knowledge of, 31; powers of, 41, 49

Shakespeare, William, 7, 72

Shame Trees Don't Grow Here (Velma Pollard), 4, 77–78

Shepherd, Verena, 113

"Sister I" (Velma Pollard), 103

slavery: abolition of, 13, 84–85, 96, 125n11; in British commonwealth countries, 36, 102; diaspora and, 64; impacts of, 16, 18–19, 110; in

Louisiana, 60–61; in *Myal*, 47, 49–50, 52; in *The Rainmaker's Mistake*, 81–91; and rebellion, 25; and trade, 11, 47, 85, 91–92, 115; in "Sleeping's Beauty and a Prince Charming," 110–11; Woodside and, 4, 6, 11–15

"Sleeping's Beauty and a Prince Charm-ing" (Erna Brodber), 108, 110–11, 113

socialism, 7, 22, 78

sociology, 6, 8–9, 53, 64, 109, 128n70

souls, 35, 53–55, 111; restoration of, 41, 42; theft of, 39, 42, 55

South America, 56, 76, 92, 131n41

space, 24, 93; Blackspace, 5–6, 18; time- and space-shifting, 21, 80, 85, 87; third, 43–44; "tomorrow's spaces," 20, 64, 72, 74–75, 79, 92

speculative fiction, 5, 13, 20, 80, 87, 92–93, 118

spirits, 4, 6–7, 14–15; ancestral, 49–50, 82; in *Homestretch*, 69; in *Louisi-ana*, 53–63; in *Myal*, 40–42, 46–52; in *The Rainmaker's Mistake*, 82, 90; Rastafarian, 38; and posses-sion, 3, 20, 39, 41, 52–53, 56, 60, 108, 114; and theft, 3, 20, 39, 40–42, 46, 48, 50–51, 114; Tayeb, 82, 90–91; trickster, 35. *See also* Anancy

spirituality, 19, 50, 57, 59; and healing, 30, 34; in *Nothing's Mat*, 92–93; in Velma Pollard's poetry, 74–75, 106. *See also* Myal (religion); Obeah

Spivak, Gayatri Chakravorty, 105

St. Mary's Parish, Jamaica, 3, 5–6, 12–13, 31, 80, 109, 111, 113–14, 117; in *Jane and Louisa Will Soon Come Home*, 31; in *Louisiana*, 52–53, 59, 62; in *Myal*, 45, 47; in *Nothing's Mat*, 96–98

strikes, 17, 53–54, 62, 78, 116, 129n78

sugar production, 12, 14, 62, 82, 111–12, 128n78
Sun Ra, 80
symbolism, 9, 23, 48, 70, 125n10

Tacky's Rebellion, 47
Taino people, 11, 19, 76, 109
Tayeb, 82, 90–91
Thibodaux Massacre, 128n78
"third space," 43–44
Tiffin, Helen, 110, 119n1, 120n22, 129n2, 135n43
time, 4, 14, 24, 57, 79, 87; narrative, 69, 102; temporal progression, 4, 118; and space-shifting, 21, 80, 85, 87, 93; traveling, 90
Tolentino, Jia, 118
"tomorrow's spaces," 20, 64, 72, 74–75, 79, 92
Toots and the Maytals, 23
Tosh, Peter, 8, 30
traditions, 11, 19, 68, 75, 93; African-derived religious, 39, 42, 45, 50; oral, 27, 74; trickster, 35, 45, 59, 73, 115–16, 124n60, 126n18, 130n26
transformation, 11, 30, 34–35, 51
transnationalism, 64, 66

unbelonging, 4, 65, 81
United Fruit Company, 16, 57, 112, 128n65
United Kingdom, 64–65, 81, 84, 92, 111, 113
United States: diaspora and, 3, 115; in Erna Brodber's writings, 13–14, 32; liberation movements in, 8, 22; in *Louisiana*, 52–53, 57, 59; Marcus Garvey and, 17; in *Nothing's Mat*, 81, 92, 98; in *The Rainmaker's Mistake*, 85, 90; Rastafarian beliefs in, 30; in Velma Pollard's writings, 10,

64–65, 70, 74, 79, 102–5, 116; Zora Neale Hurston and, 9
Universal Negro Improvement Association (UNIA), 16–17, 59–60, 126n28
universities, 5, 24; in *Homestretch*, 65; in *Karl*, 27, 32–33; in *Louisiana*, 52, 59; in *Nothing's Mat*, 92, 96, 98; in *The Rainmaker's Mistake*, 89; teacher training colleges, 16, 51; women in, 100
University of Sussex, 8
University of the West Indies at Mona (UWI), 4–5, 7, 27, 33, 92, 96
University of Washington, 7

"Virgin Island Suite" (Velma Pollard), 75
Virgin Islands, 10, 65, 74–77
Vodun, 55
voodoo, 9, 15, 39, 50, 52–53, 55, 57, 61, 128n61

Wailer, Bunny, 8
Walcott, Derek, 73
Ward, Martha, 128n61
Waters, Anita M., 121n5
Wellesley College, 8
West Indies, 57, 67, 95
whiteness: in "Gran," 108; in *Karl*, 25, 27; in *Myal*, 41–43, 46, 49; in *The Rainmaker's Mistake*, 81; "white Jamaican," 43, 125n12; "The White Man's Burden," 43, 46, 125n11
Witch of Endor, 48, 61, 126n33
Womack, Ytasha L., 80, 131n2, 132n3
women: Black, 63–64, 110, 114; in Erna Brodber's writings, 108–13; feminism, 9; Jamaican, 21, 68, 100, 103, 116; and liberation movements, 8; in *Louisiana*, 53, 55–56, 60, 63;

matriarch, 108; in *Myal*, 39, 41–42, 44, 46–47; in *Nothing's Mat*, 97; in sisters' writings, 9, 31, 100–101, 114–16; wives, 106; in Velma Pollard's writings, 10, 68, 73, 75–77, 101, 103–7; womanhood, 108–10

wood, 84–85

Woodside, Jamaica: in Erna Brodber's writings, 11–16, 109; histories of, 12–14, 16, 18–20; in *Homestretch*, 65–66; in *Jane and Louisa Will Soon Come Home*, 32, 34, 38; in *Karl*, 25, 27; in *Louisiana*, 52; in *Myal*, 44; in *The Rainmaker's Mistake*, 80, 91; and sisters' background, 3–7, 16, 18–20, 113, 117; in Velma Pollard's writings, 9, 72;

"Writing Your Village History—the Case of Woodside," 6, 12

Woodside, Pear Tree Grove P.O. (Erna Brodber), 6, 11, 13–15, 18

working class, 78, 101, 113

World Is a High Hill, The (Erna Brodber), 5, 100, 111–13

World War II, 28, 58, 66

"Writing Your Village History—the Case of Woodside" (Erna Brodber), 6, 12

"Xunantunich" (Velma Pollard), 76–77

Yale University, 5

yams, 13, 57, 112; in *The Rainmaker's Mistake*, 80–84, 86–90

Yards in the City of Kingston (Erna Brodber), 8

ABOUT THE AUTHOR

Violet Harrington Bryan is a Professor Emerita of English at Xavier University of Louisiana. She is a native of Florence, South Carolina, and received her BA from Mount Holyoke College in South Hadley, Massachusetts, and her MA and PhD from Harvard University. She published *The Myth of New Orleans in Literature: Dialogues of Race and Gender* (University of Tennessee Press, 1993) and has written articles on African American and Caribbean writers. She has taught courses in African American literature and world literature and seminars on Women Writers of the Caribbean and the Diaspora, Medicine and Literature, and Writers of New Orleans.